ISBN 978-0-265-70206-2
PIBN 10060027

# THE BROKEN HEART

BY

## JOHN FORD

EDITED WITH

*NOTES AND INTRODUCTION*

BY

## CLINTON SCOLLARD

*Professor of English Literature in Hamilton College*

NEW YORK

## HENRY HOLT AND COMPANY

1895

*12-322*

THE MERSHON COMPANY PRESS,
RAHWAY, N. J.

# INTRODUCTION.

## I.

THE most patient and persistent search into the lives of the old English dramatists is often but meagerly rewarded. Wide and perplexing gaps must be filled by the imagination, or, as it were, a fitting garment of fancy fashioned for the bare and broken skeleton of fact. Such is the case with John Ford. The dramatist was the second son of Thomas Ford, his mother being the sister of John Popham, Lord Chief Justice under James I. The Ford family was one of good standing in Devonshire, where, at Ilsington, John Ford was baptized on the 17th of April, 1586. What schooling he had was obtained in or near his native town. If he went to either of the great universities he could hardly have remained more than one or two terms, for he was enrolled as a member of the Middle Temple in November, 1602. Popham had been appointed treasurer of this organization twenty years earlier, and it has been conjectured that he took an active interest in his young relative. A cousin and namesake had preceded the poet in London as a member of Gray's Inn, and between the two there appears to have existed an intimacy and affection almost brotherly. Though he retained his connection with the Temple, there is no evidence to show that Ford was ever called to the bar. In addressing his patrons, several of whom were men of rank, he not infrequently alludes to his determination not to allow his ambitions as a dramatist to interfere with his regular occupation. From this it is seen that he did not depend upon play-writing for support. It has been inferred that he looked after the legal interests of large landed estates, doubtless acting as advisor in matters requiring a knowledge of jurisprudence. A line in the prologue to the comedy, *Fancies Chaste and Noble*, has led some to conclude that at the time the play was produced the author was probably traveling upon the Continent, but there is no proof that he ever crossed the Channel. In regard to his retirement from London, and his death, nothing very satisfactory can be stated. It is commonly affirmed that he withdrew from the Temple in 1639, and that he then sought his native town, having amassed a considerable fortune, and thinking to pass the remainder of his life in quiet. According to one tradition he married and had children, but this is hardly to be credited. The troublous times which followed his withdrawal from the active world obscured much that otherwise would be clear. It is quite possible that Ford was in his grave before the oncoming of these evil days, but if he was not, the stress of events was sufficient to veil the close of his life, like that of many another, in oblivion.

Of the dramatist's personality almost nothing is known. Because his fancy led him to the choice of somber themes it has been assumed that he was of a melancholy temperament. This idea has been strengthened by the often quoted couplet from a contemporary rhymer :

" Deep in a dump John Ford was alone got (gat).
With folded arms and melancholy hat."

This, however, may have been intended simply as a caricature. The idea that an early love-affair, referred to in *Fame's Memorial*, may have influenced him deeply, and induced a settled moodiness, may, with safety, be dismissed. Poets, and especially young poets, have always been prone to prate of their imaginary blighted hopes, and Ford's " flint-hearted Lycia " probably caused him little more than a passing pang, if, in fact, she ever actually existed. But that Ford's mind was of a serious cast his curious little manual for every day conduct, *The Line of Life*, abundantly proves. He appears to have been upon reasonably good terms with his fellow playwrights and poets, as several commendatory verses upon his plays by such men as Crashaw and Shirley are extant, and Ford himself was one of those who burst into mourning song at the death of Ben Jonson, whom he saw fit to style " the best of English poets."

## II.

Although Ford may be said to represent the period of dramatic decline, it is indeed a splendid decadence that can boast of such plays as Massinger's *Maid of Honour*, Shirley's *Traitor*, and Ford's *Broken Heart.* Compared with the best work of the Restoration playwrights these dramas are of the very highest order. It is only when we contrast them with the plays of the master dramatist of all time that their true middle position is established.

So far as we know, Ford first challenged public recognition as a poet in 1606 with his *Fame's Memorial,* an elegiac poem of considerable length upon Charles Blount, Earl of Devonshire. Why the young poet singled out this nobleman for the subject of his ingenious stanzas we cannot say. Blount, though a man of much prominence, had died in disgrace, and it does not appear that Ford was acquainted either with him or with the countess to whom he dedicated his elegiacs in a hopelessly involved acrostic, "the worst," according to Gifford, "that ever passed the press." There is nothing whatever here to presage the future dramatist. A command of measure and of poetic phraseology indicates, however, that the author had served his apprenticeship. According to the dramatist's own statement his play, *The Lover's Melancholy,* published in 1629, was "the first of his that ever courted reader." But during the twenty-three years that intervened between the appearance of *Fame's Memorial* and this piece, he certainly had been heard upon the stage, if not read in the closet. Indeed it is highly probable that his name, though in conjunction with others, had been seen upon the title-page of dramas now lost. There are extant seven plays entirely of Ford's composition, and an additional two in which he assisted, Decker being his collaborator in one instance, and Rowley and Decker in the other. At least four more are entered under his name upon the Stationer's books, and the titles of three others in which he had a hand have been preserved. Assuming that these dramas constitute the entire bulk of his labors (which is not probable), we have, by which to judge him, something more than half of his actual production. On the theory, perhaps, of the survival of the fittest, it has been argued that the best of his work has come down to us, and it may be that this is a safe presumption.

Ford's masterpiece is unquestionably *The Broken Heart*, and whether it merits the somewhat extravagant praise bestowed upon it by Charles Lamb, it certainly sets before us in a vivid way some of the most powerful human emotions : love, sorrow, hatred, and despair. Fewer of the dramatist's prevailing faults are here evident than in any other of his plays save *Perkin Warbeck*. He may not rise to such heights in single scenes, or in detached passages, as elsewhere, but in general effect he is more harmonious and powerful. " Mock pathos " is one of the most serious charges that has been urged against Ford, and though it be granted that in some instances the tenderness may seem strained, and the agony prolonged with melodramatic intent, these objections do not hold against the portrayal of the sorrows of Calantha and the woes of Penthea. In the prologue the dramatist is careful to state that the story

" When Time's youth
Wanted some riper years, was known a Truth."

It is, however, certain that he did not draw the tale from historical sources. Prolific as Sparta may have

been in tragedies, it never was the scene of this one.
If, as Ford says, the incidents were not of his own invention, he doubtless found them, or the suggestions
from which the plot grew, in the now lost romance
of some Spanish or Italian writer.  What seems not
improbable is that, like many another author since, he
sought to add to the effect of his fiction by boldly
claiming a basis of fact for it.  At least he merits high
praise for the elaboration, the skillful fitting together,
the general working out of the whole.  He expended
much more pains upon details than was common with
him.  The subordinate characters are more fully and
carefully developed, and the scenes follow one another
with a more natural sequence.  Then, too, the mo-
ments of passion, of the poet's fine frenzy, are more
frequent than in other plays.  There is far less that is
evidently studied.  Ford is not a poet who often gives
us the impression of having struck off a scene or an
act at white heat.  We are too likely to feel that his
is the work of the cunning-craftsman who has weighed
and calculated the effect of word, line, and passage.
But this is not so in the case of *The Broken Heart.*
Here there is something more than the most perfect
artifice, that fine touch of the emotions of which we are
so frequently and so thrillingly conscious in reading
Shakespere, and which we too often just miss in
Ford.

Ford's other tragedies, *'Tis Pity She's a Whore* and
*Love's Sacrifice,* are not likely to attract the casual
reader, but to the student of the dramatist both are
interesting.  Unfortunate in title and revolting in
subject as is the first-named play, it is not fair to

Ford for us to allow our natural prejudice against it to obscure its manifest merits. The drama unquestionably contains some of the author's strongest writing. The story, taken, like that of *Love's Sacrifice*, from an Italian source, tells of a brother and sister who conceive a mad passion for one another, and abandon themselves with what Jeffrey calls "a splendid and perverted devotedness" to their unlawful loves. Ultimately the sister is forced into marriage, and the husband discovers his wife's guilt. What could arise from so horrible a situation save despair, frenzy, and murder?—a fitting close for so dreadful a chapter of events. The question likely to suggest itself after the perusal of this awful tragedy is—should such a succession of scenes be made the subject of the playwright's art? It has been said, "better no dramas at all than those with such disgusting themes!" an opinion with which one is inclined to concur. Yet it must be granted that Ford has managed the plot both with dexterity and dignity, considering the delicate matter he has in hand. While we turn from Giovanni with repulsion and loathing, toward the unfortunate and distracted Arabella our sympathies are unconsciously drawn. In the scene where the sister meets death from her brother's dagger the dramatist reaches the climax of tragic power. No passage from any of the old playwrights, save certain memorable ones in Shakespere and two or three in Webster, conveys more of what might be termed the inevitableness of doom than this.

Few graces save those of expression are discoverable in *Love's Sacrifice,* while all of Ford's most prom-

inent faults are evident.   On Bianca, the most con-
spicuous female character, not a little false sentiment
is wasted.   Though not in act a traitor to her husband,
she certainly is so at heart, yet toward the close of the
play she is spoken of as living " a life of innocence
and beauty."   The whole situation is inconceivable.
A woman, at first represented as deeply attached to
her husband, suddenly and without apparent reason
is seized with a violent infatuation for another.   The
other, up to this moment fervent and ardent in the
protestations of his passion, is all at once as " chaste
as ice."   The husband's jealousy is basely aroused,
and a sanguinary sequel is the result.   Not only is the
main thread of this play exceedingly ill-woven, but
the tangled underplot, in which Ford is rarely fortunate, is here more than usually lacking in refinement.

*Perkin Warbeck*, Ford's one history or chronicle
play, stands easily second to *The Broken Heart* in
clearness of outline, carefulness of detail, and com-
pleteness of general conception.   It is one of the few
dramas of its class that will bear comparison with
Shakespere's matchless transcripts from the actual
life of the past.   The hero is the best male character
we have from Ford's pen.   Whatever the young pre-
tender to the English throne may really have been,
we behold, in the dramatist's portrait of him, a noble
youth of single purpose, who believes implicity in his
right to the crown, and who goes to his death main-
taining that right.   There is no inconsistency in the
poet's picture.   Warbeck enlists our sympathies at the
outset, and our interest in him never flags through all
his vicissitudes until he gives up his life on Tower Hill.

We are not surprised that the charming Lady Katherine listens so readily to his avowals, for in him appear to be united the gallantry of the lover, the dignity of the rightful sovereign, and the tenderness and valiant manliness of the true gentleman. Here, too, as in Ford's masterpiece, the lesser characters are well defined—the just and genial Huntley, the leal and brave Daryell, the vacillating Scotch monarch, all, in fact, show the same painstaking execution. This is a canvas whose minor, as well as whose major, figures will bear the closest scrutiny.

Of Ford's three romantic comedies *The Lover's Melancholy* is clearly the best ; and while the play is by no means a strong one, there is much about it that is singularly attractive. In spite of the slight reminiscences it betrays of Beaumont and Fletcher's *Philaster*, there is but little exaggeration in the statement that here Ford has met and equaled his brother dramatists in their own chosen field. It would seem as though the poet had deliberately, at times, retarded the rapid development of the plot in order to beautify the story. Nowhere else does Ford give a hint of what he might have accomplished had he attempted narrative verse writing. His apparently keen sense of the romantic surprises us ; not so, however, his touches of pathos, though these are of a far softer and less harrowing nature than in *The Broken Heart*. Insanity was something that most of the Elizabethans from Kyd downward were fond of attempting to portray, and sorry work many of them made of it. Ford can hardly be said to approach Shakespere in this particular, or possibly even Webster in that notable scene in *The White Devil* (Cornelia at the bier of Marcello), but Penthea demented is not so far removed from Ophelia, and old Meleander in *The Lover's Melancholy*, with mind unbalanced through grief at the supposed death of his favorite daughter, is vastly above the ordinary stage madman. The chief male characters in this play lack stamina, and are little better than lackadaisical, moon-struck lovers. Ford's genius was not of the masculine type like that of Massinger. Except Perkin Warbeck, and a few others, his men are either coxcombs or weaklings, somehow wanting in strong moral force. It is in the delineation of the female character that we find Ford in his element. His knowledge of the motives, the springs of action, that move the feminine heart was both deep and intimate. Among the most attractive of his women are the sisters Eroclea and Cleophila in *The Lover's Melancholy*. Neither, strictly speaking, is of the heroic mold, but both are thoroughly natural and charming. Eroclea, in spite of her youth's disguise and her assumed mannishness, is naïve and fascinating, with a dash of real bravery, while Cleophila's devotion to her insane father is especially touching. A different quality of devotion, and one that excites our admiration more keenly, is that shown by Katherine Gordon to her husband, Perkin Warbeck. Whatever the world may say of him, her belief in his truth and honor is not to be shaken, and he goes to his execution strengthened by her loving faith. Penthea's patient endurance and Calantha's sublime stoicism combine to make "a monument of sorrows" that has few counterparts on the pages of tragedy. Arabella, despite the terrible character of her guilt, moves to pity, and even in Bianca, Ford's one signal failure in his portrayal of femineity, when we have once accepted the impossible change that comes over her, there is something finely daring. It is a misguided heroism which leads her to tell her husband to his face that, while she is true to him, she holds Fernando infinitely above him as a man, but it is heroism nevertheless. To the gallery of Ford's heroines two others might be added, Spinella from *The Lady's Trial* and Castamela from *Fancies Chaste and Noble*, characters whose purity and charm serve to relieve the dullness of two poorly constructed and otherwise objectionable plays. Ford's conception of woman was upon a vastly higher plane than the view taken of her by his contemporaries, and it is only in the pages of Shakespere that we meet with braver, more refined, and loftier types.

Gifford's characterization of Ford's humor as "a dull medley of extravagance and impurity" is not inapt. Surely poet never wrote who lacked to a greater degree the true sense of the humorous, yet who persisted in introducing characters intended to be comic. In some of the plays the alleged comicalities are not offensive, as in the case of the rival lovers, Guzman and Fulgoso, in *The Lady's Trial*. Their fun consists in strutting both with legs and tongue, and in berating one another most roundly when they can find no one else to abuse. Too often, however, inoffensive is a term that cannot be applied to Ford's intended pleasantries. The dramatist who could end the death agonies of several of his most prominent characters with a long drawn out " O—O " must have been quite as sadly lacking in the sense of the ridiculous as the noted seer and singer who wrote :

> " Only the ass with motion dull
> Upon the pivot of his skull
> Turned round his long left ear."

Ford's diction is uniformly felicitous. Unless it be Beaumont and Fletcher, no dramatists of his day have a greater grace of phrase. He caught from Shakespere, perhaps, the art of vivifying a whole paragraph by a single daring metaphor or verbal transposition, erring sometimes in taste, to be sure, but generally effecting his end. Even into the mouths of some of his most senseless comic characters he occasionally puts such happy turns of expression as these :

> " Her fair eyes
> Like to a pair of pointed beams drawn from
> The sun's most glorious orb, do dazzle sight,
> Audacious to gaze there : then over those
> A several bow of jet securely twines
> In semicircles; under them two banks
> Of roses red and white, divided by
> An arch of polished ivory, surveying
> A temple from whence oracles proceed
> More gracious than Apollo's, more desired
> Than amorous songs of poets, softly tuned."

Ford's rendering of the classical legend of the musical strife between the nightingale and the musician, introduced into the first act of *The Lover's Melancholy*, will further serve to illustrate the rare harmony and beauty of diction of which he was capable :

            " One morning early
This accident encountered me : I heard
The sweetest and most ravishing contention
That art and nature ever were at strife in.

A sound of music touched my ears, or rather
Indeed entranced my soul.   As I stole nearer,
Invited by the melody, I saw
This youth, this fair-faced youth, upon his lute,
With strains of strange variety and harmony,
Proclaiming, as it seemed, so bold a challenge
To the clear choristers of the woods, the birds,
That, as they flocked about him, all stood silent.
               . . . A nightingale,
Nature's best-skilled musician, undertakes
The challenge, and for every several strain
The well-shaped youth could touch, she sung her own :
He could not run division with more art
Upon his quaking instrument than she,
The nightingale, did with her various notes
Reply to : . . .
Some time thus spent, the young man grew at last
Into a pretty anger, that a bird,
Whom art had never taught clefs, moods, or notes,
Should vie with him for mastery, whose study
Had busied many hours to perfect practice :
To end the controversy, in a rapture
Upon his instrument he plays so swiftly,
So many voluntaries and so quick,
That there was curiosity and cunning,
Concord in discord, lines of differing method
Meeting in one full center of delight.
            . . . The bird, ordained to be
Music's first martyr, strove to imitate
These several sounds ; which when her warbling throat
Failed in, for grief down dropped she on his lute,
And brake her heart.   It was the quaintest sadness,

To see the conqueror upon her hearse
To weep a funeral elegy of tears ;

    .      .      .      .      .

      He looked upon the trophies of his art,
Then sighed, then wiped his eyes, then sighed and cried,
' Alas, poor creature ! I will soon revenge
This cruelty upon the author of it ;
Henceforth this lute, guilty of innocent blood,
Shall never more betray a harmless peace
To an untimely end : ' and in that sorrow,
And as he was pashing it against a tree,
I suddenly stept in."

Though Winstanley states that Ford's plays were profitable to the managers of the theaters where they were produced, it is difficult to believe that he was ever a popular writer.  In the garden of his fancy he cultivated too many mournful blossoms, the rue, the night-shade, and the

        " Amaranth, flower of Death."

The ways of sorrow he made his own, and the children of grief were his familiars.  Where the forest shades of woe were deepest the sound of that delicate instrument, his lute, was natural, plaintive, melancholy, pity-evoking, but in the mirthful sunlight it was too often strained and out of tune.  We can but think of Ford's muse as of one sad-eyed and lorn,

        " Like Niobe, all tears."

Touching at certain points, now Shakespere, now Marston, now Beaumont and Fletcher, and most resembling the gloom-enshrouded Webster in the bent of his genius, he yet stands apart from them all, an isolated figure, wrapped in the mantle of his darkly contemplative temperament.

Thou cheat'st us, Ford : mak'st one seem two by art :
What is Love's Sacrifice but the Broken Heart ?

RICHARD CRASHAW.

# PROLOGUE.

OUR scene is Sparta.   He whose best of art
Hath drawn this piece calls it THE BROKEN HEART.
The title lends no expectation here
Of apish laughter, or of some lame jeer
At place or persons ; no pretended clause          5
Of jests fit for a brothel court's applause
From vulgar admiration : such low songs,
Tuned to unchaste ears, suit not modest tongues.
The virgin-sisters then deserved fresh bays
When innocence and sweetness crowned their lays ;
Then vices gasped for breath, whose whole com-
     mérce                                              11
Was whipped to exile by unblushing verse.
This law we keep in our presentment now,
Not to take freedom more than we allow ;
What may be here thought Fiction, when Time's youth
Wanted some riper years, was known a Truth :   16
In which, if words have clothed the subject right,
You may partake a pity with delight.

# DRAMATIS PERSONÆ.

AMYCLAS, King of Laconia.
ITHOCLES, a Favourite.
ORGILUS, Son of Crotolon.
BASSANES, a jealous Nobleman.
ARMOSTES, a Counsellor of State.
CROTOLON, another Counsellor.
PROPHILUS, Friend of Ithocles.
NEARCHUS, Prince of Argos.
TECNICUS, a Philosopher.
HEMOPHIL, } Courtiers.
GRONEAS, }
AMELUS, Friend of Nearchus.
PHULAS, Servant to Bassanes.
Lords, Courtiers, Officers, Attendants, &c.


CALANTHA, Daughter of Amyclas.
PENTHEA, Sister of Ithocles and Wife of Bassanes.
EUPHRANEA, Daughter of Crotolon, a Maid of honour.
CHRISTALLA, } Maids of honour.
PHILEMA, }
GRAUSIS, Overseer of Penthea.


SCENE—SPARTA.

# THE BROKEN HEART.

## ACT THE FIRST.

SCENE I.   *A Room in* CROTOLON'S *House.*

*Enter* CROTOLON *and* ORGILUS.

*Crot.*   Dally not further ; I will know the reason
That speeds thee to this journey.

*Org.*                                        Reason ! good sir,
I can yield many.

*Crot.*                    Give me one, a good one ;
Such I expect, and ere we part must have :
Athens ! pray, why to Athens ? you intend not          5
To kick against the world, turn cynic, stoic,
Or read the logic-lecture, or become
An Areopagite, and judge in cases
Touching the commonwealth ; for, as I take it,
The budding of your chin cannot prognosticate         10
So grave an honour.

*Org.*                    All this I acknowledge.

*Crot.*   You do ! then, son, if books and love of
   knowledge
Inflame you to this travel, here in Sparta
You may as freely study.

*Org.*                         'Tis not that, sir.

*Crot.* Not that, sir ! As a father, I command thee
T' acquaint me with the truth.

*Org.* Thus I obey ye. 16
After so many quarrels as dissension,
Fury, and rage had broached in blood, and sometimes
With death to such confederates as sided
With now-dead Thrasus and yourself, my lord ; 20
Our present king, Amyclas, reconciled
Your eager swords and sealed a gentle peace ;
Friends you professed yourselves ; which to confirm,
A resolution for a lasting league
Betwixt your families was entertained, 25
By joining in a Hymenean bond
Me and the fair Penthea, only daughter
To Thrasus.

*Crot.* What of this ?

*Org.* Much, much, dear sir.
A freedom of convérse, an interchange
Of holy and chaste love, so fixed our souls 30
In a firm growth of union, that no time
Can eat into the pledge : we had enjoyed
The sweets our vows expected, had not cruelty
Prevented all those triumphs we prepared for,
By Thrasus his untimely death.

*Crot.* Most certain. 35

*Org.* From this time sprouted-up that poisonous
stalk
Of aconite, whose ripened fruit hath ravished
All health, all comfort of a happy life ;
For Ithocles, her brother, proud of youth,
And prouder in his power, nourished closely 40

The memory of former discontents,
To glory in revenge.   By cunning partly,
Partly by threats, he woos at once, and forces
His virtuous sister to admit a marriage
With Bassanes, a nobleman, in honour                    45
And riches, I confess, beyond my fortunes.

   *Crot.*   All this is no sound reason to impórtune
My leave for thy departure.

   *Org.*                              Now it follows
Beauteous Penthea, wedded to this torture
By an insulting brother, being secretly                 50
Compelled to yield her virgin freedom up
To him, who never can usurp her heart,
Before contracted mine, is now so yoked
To a most barbarous thraldom, misery,
Affliction, that he savours not humanity,               55
Whose sorrow melts not into more than pity
In hearing but her name.

   *Crot.*                          As how, pray ?

   *Org.*                                Bassanes,
The man that calls her wife, considers truly
What heaven of perfections he is lord of
By thinking fair Penthea his : this thought             60
Begets a kind of monster-love, which love
Is nurse unto a fear so strong and servile
As brands all dotage with a jealousy :
All eyes who gaze upon that shrine of beauty
He doth resolve do homage to the miracle ;              65
Some one, he is assured, may now or then,
If opportunity but sort, prevail :
So much, out of a self-unworthiness,

His fears transport him ; not that he finds cause
In her obedience, but his own distrust.　　　70

　*Crot.*　You spin out your discourse.

　*Org.*　　　　　　My griefs are violent :
For, knowing how the maid was heretofore
Courted by me, his jealousies grow wild
That I should steal again into her favours,
And undermine her virtues ; which the gods　　75
Know I nor dare nor dream of.　Hence, from hence,
I undertake a voluntary exile ;
First, by my absence to take off the cares.
Of jealous Bassanes ; but chiefly, sir,
To free Penthea from a hell on earth ;　　80
Lastly, to lose the memory of something
Her presence makes to live in me afresh.

　*Crot.*　Enough, my Orgilus, enough.　To Athens,
I give a full consent.—Alas, good lady !—
We shall hear from thee often ?

　*Org.*　　　　　　Often.

　*Crot.*　　　　　　　　　See,　85
Thy sister comes to give a farewell.

*Enter* EUPHRANEA.

　*Euph.*　　　　　　Brother !

　*Org.*　Euphranea, thus upon thy cheeks I print
A brother's kiss ; more careful of thine honour,
Thy health, and thy well-doing, than my life.
Before we part, in presence of our father,　　90
I must prefer a suit t' ye.

　*Euph.*　　　　　You may style it,
My brother, a command.

*Org.*               That you will promise
Never to pass to any man, however
Worthy, your faith, till, with our father's leave,
I give a free consent.

*Crot.*           An easy motion !       95
I'll promise for her, Orgilus.

*Org.*             Your pardon ;
Euphranea's oath must yield me satisfaction.

*Euph.*   By Vesta's sacred fires I swear.

*Crot.*                  And I,
By great Apollo's beams, join in the vow,
Not without thy allowance to bestow her      100
On any living.

*Org.*        Dear Euphranea,
Mistake me not : far, far 'tis from my thought,
As far from any wish of mine, to hinder
Preferment to an honourable bed
Or fitting fortune ; thou art young and handsome ;
And 'twere injustice,—more, a tyranny,—      106
Not to advance thy merit : trust me, sister,
It shall be my first care to see thee matched
As may become thy choice and our contents.
I have your oath.

*Euph.*       You have. But mean you, brother,
To leave us, as you say ?

*Crot.*           Ay, ay, Euphranea :    111
He has just grounds direct him. I will prove
A father and a brother to thee.

*Euph.*          Heaven
Does look into the secrets of all hearts :
Gods, you have mercy with ye, else—

*Crot.*                    Doubt nothing;   115
Thy brother will return in safety to us.

*Org.*   Souls sunk in sorrows never are without 'em;
They change fresh airs, but bear their griefs about 'em.

                                        [*Exeunt.*

### SCENE II.   *A Room in the Palace.*

*Flourish.   Enter* AMYCLAS, ARMOSTES, PROPHILUS,
Courtiers, *and* Attendants.

*Amy.*   The Spartan gods are gracious; our humility
Shall bend before their altars, and perfume
Their temples with abundant sacrifice.
See, lords, Amyclas, your old king, is entering
Into his youth again ! I shall shake off            5
This silver badge of age, and change this snow
For hairs as gay as are Apollo's locks ;
Our heart leaps in new vigour.

*Arm.*                         May old time
Run back to double your long life, great sir !

*Amy.*   It will, it must, Armostes: thy bold nephew,
Death-braving Ithocles, brings to our gates            11
Triumphs and peace upon his conquering sword.
Laconia is a monarchy at length ;
Hath in this latter war trod under foot
Messene's pride ; Messene bows her neck            15
To Lacedæmon's royalty.   O, 'twas
A glorious victory, and doth deserve
More than a chronicle—a temple, lords,
A temple to the name of Ithocles.—
Where didst thou leave him, Prophilus ?

*Pro.*                          At Pephon, 20

Most gracious sovereign ; twenty of the noblest
Of the Messenians there attend your pleasure,
For such conditions as you shall propose
In settling peace, and liberty of life.

*Amy.* When comes your friend the general ?

*Pro.* He promised
To follow with all speed convenient. 26

*Enter* CALANTHA, EUPHRANEA ; CHRISTALLA *and*
PHILEMA *with a garland ; and* CROTOLON.

*Amy.* Our daughter !—Dear Calantha, the happy
_ news,
The conquest of Messene, hath already
Enriched thy knowledge.

*Cal.* With the circumstance
And manner of the fight, related faithfully 30
By Prophilus himself.—But, pray, sir, tell me
How doth the youthful general demean
His actions in these fortunes?

*Pro.* Excellent princess,
Your own fair eyes may soon report a truth
Unto your judgment, with what moderation, 35
Calmness of nature, measure, bounds, and limits
Of thankfulness and joy, he doth digest
Such amplitude of his success as would
In others, moulded of a spirit less clear,
Advance 'em to comparison with heaven : 40
But Ithocles—

*Cal.* Your friend—

*Pro.* He is so, madam,
In which the period of my fate consists :

He, in this firmament of honour, stands
Like a star fixed, not moved with any thunder
Of popular applause or sudden lightning       45
Of self-opinion ; he hath served his country,
And thinks 'twas but his duty.

   *Crot.*               You describe
A miracle of man.

   *Amy.*          Such, Crotolon,
On forfeit of a king's word, thou wilt find him.—

                         [*Flourish.*
Hark, warning of his coming ! all attend him.       50

*Enter* ITHOCLES, *ushered in by the* Lords, *and followed*
      *by* HEMOPHIL *and* GRONEAS.

Return into these arms, thy home, thy sanctuary,
Delight of Sparta, treasure of my bosom,
Mine own, own Ithocles !

   *Ith.*             Your humblest subject.

   *Arm.*  Proud of the blood I claim an interest in,
As brother to thy mother, I embrace thee,       55
Right noble nephew.

   *Ith.*             Sir, your love's too partial.

   *Crot.*  Our country speaks by me, who by thy valour,
Wisdom, and service, shares in this great action ;
Returning thee, in part of thy due merits,
A general welcome.

   *Ith.*             You exceed in bounty.       60

   *Cal.*  Christalla, Philema, the chaplet. [*Takes the*
   *chaplet from them.*]—Ithocles,
Upon the wings of fame the singular

And chosen fortune of an high attempt
Is borne so past the view of common sight,
That I myself with mine own hands have wrought,  65
To crown thy temples, this provincial garland :
Accept, wear, and enjoy it as our gift
Deserved, not purchased.

    *Ith.*                 You're a royal maid.

    *Amy.*   She is in all our daughter.

    *Ith.*                    Let me blush,
Acknowledging how poorly I have served,       70
What nothings I have done, compared with the
    honours
Heaped on the issue of a willing mind ;
In that lay mine ability, that only ;
For who is he so sluggish from his birth,
So little worthy of a name or country,         75
That owes not out of gratitude for life
A debt of service, in what kind soever
Safety or counsel of the commonwealth
Requires, for payment ?

    *Cal.*         He speaks truth.

    *Ith.*                Whom heaven
Is pleased to style victorious, there to such    80
Applause runs madding, like the drunken priests
In Bacchus' sacrifices, without reason
Voicing the leader-on a demi-god ;
Whenas, indeed, each common soldier's blood
Drops down as current coin in that hard purchase  85
As his whose much more delicate condition
Hath sucked the milk of ease ; judgment commands,
But resolution executes.  I use not,

Before this royal presence, these fit slights
As in contempt of such as can direct ;                    90
My speech hath other end ; not to attribute
All praise to one man's fortune, which is strengthened
By many hands : for instance, here is Prophilus,
A gentleman—I cannot flatter truth—
Of much desert ; and, though in other rank,           95
Both Hemophil and Groneas were not missing
To wish their country's peace ; for, in a word,
All there did strive their best, and 'twas our duty.

 *Amy.* Courtiers turn soldiers !—We vouchsafe our
  hand.
   [HEMOPHIL *and* GRONEAS *kiss his hand.*
Observe your great example.

 *Hem.*      With all diligence.

 *Gro.* Obsequiously and hourly.

 *Amy.*      Some repose  101
After these toils is needful.  We must think on
Conditions for the conquered ; they expect 'em.
On !—Come, my Ithocles.

 *Euph.*    Sir, with your favour,
I need not a supporter.

 *Pro.*    Fate instructs me.        105
   [*Exit* AMYCLAS *attended,* ITHOCLES, CA-
   LANTHA, etc.  *As* CHRISTALLA *and* PHI-
   LEMA *are following* CALANTHA *they are
   detained by* HEMOPHIL *and* GRONEAS.

 *Chris.* With me ?
 *Phil.*    Indeed I dare not stay.

*Hem.* Sweet lady.
Soldiers are blunt,—your lip. [*Kisses her.*

 *Chris.* Fie, this is rudeness :
You went not hence such creatures.

 *Gro.* Spirit of valour
Is of a mounting nature.

 *Phil.* It appears so.—
In earnest, pray, how many men apiece   110
Have you two been the death of ?

 *Gro.* 'Faith, not many ;
We were composed of mercy.

 *Hem.* For our daring,
You heard the general's approbation
Before the king.

 *Chris.* You " wished your country's peace ";
That showed your charity : where are your spoils, 115
Such as the soldier fights for ?

 *Phil.* They are coming.

 *Chris.* By the next carrier, are they not ?

 *Gro.* Sweet Philema,
When I was in the thickest of mine enemies,
Slashing off one man's head, another's nose,
Another's arms and legs,—

 *Phil.* And all together.  120

 *Gro.* Then would I with a sigh remember thee,
And cry " Dear Philema, 'tis for thy sake
I do these deeds of wonder ! "—dost not love me
With all thy heart now ?

 *Phil.* Now as heretofore.

I have not put my love to use ; the principal          125
Will hardly yield an interest.

*Gro.*                          By Mars,
I'll marry thee !

*Phil.*          By Vulcan, you're forsworn,
Except my mind do alter strangely.

*Gro.*                          One word.

*Chris.*   You lie beyond all modesty :—forbear me.

*Hem.*   I'll make thee mistress of a city ; 'tis          130
Mine own by conquest.

*Chris.*                  By petition ; sue for't
*In formâ pauperis.*—City ! kennel.—Gallants !
Off with your feathers, put on aprons, gallants ;
Lear to reel, thrum, or trim a lady's dog,
And be good quiet souls of peace, hobgoblins !          135

*Hem.*   Christalla !

*Chris.*                  Practise to drill hogs, in hope
To share in the acorns.—Soldiers ? corncutters,
But not so valiant ; they ofttimes draw blood,
Which you durst never do.  When you have practised
More wit or more civility, we'll rank ye          140
I' the list of men ; till then, brave things-at-arms,
Dare not to speak to us,—most potent Groneas !—

*Phil.*   And Hemophil the hardy !—at your services.
                  [*Exeunt* CHRISTALLA *and* PHILEMA.

*Gro.*   They scorn us, as they did before we went.

*Hem.*   Hang 'em ! let us scorn them, and be
     revenged.          145

*Gro.*   Shall we ?

*Hem.* We will : and when we slight them thus,
Instead of following them, they'll follow us ;
It is a woman's nature.

*Gro.* 'Tis a scurvy one. [*Exeunt.*


SCENE III. *The Gardens of the Palace. A Grove.*

*Enter* TECNICUS, *and* ORGILUS *disguised like one of his* Scholars.

*Tec.* Tempt not the stars ; young man, thou canst
   not play
With the severity of fate : this change
Of habit and disguise in outward view
Hides not the secrets of thy soul within thee
From their quick-piercing eyes, which dive at all times
Down to thy thoughts : in thy aspéct I note          6
A consequence of danger.

*Org.* Give me leave,
Grave Tecnicus, without foredooming destiny,
Under thy roof to ease my silent griefs,
By applying to my hidden wounds the balm          10
Of thy oraculous lectures. If my fortune
Run such a crookèd by-way as to wrest
My steps to ruin, yet thy learnèd precepts
Shall call me back and set my footings straight.
I will not court the world.

*Tec.* Ah, Orgilus,          15
Neglects in young men of delights and life
Run often to extremities ; they care not
For harms to others who contemn their own.

*Org.* But I, most learnèd artist, am not so much

At odds with nature that I grudge the thrift        20
Of any true deserver ; nor doth malice
Of present hopes so check them with despair
As that I yield to thought of more affliction
Than what is incident to frailty : wherefore
Impute not this retirèd course of living        25
Some little time to any other cause
Than what I justly render,—the information
Of an unsettled mind ; as the effect
Must clearly witness.

    *Tec.*              Spirit of truth inspire thee !
On these conditions I conceal thy change,        30
And willingly admit thee for an auditor.—
I'll to my study.

    *Org.*        I to contemplations
In these delightful walks.       [*Exit* TECNICUS.
                       Thus metamorphosed,
I may without suspicion harken after
Penthea's usage and Euphranea's faith.        35
Love, thou art full of mystery ! the deities
Themselves are not secure in searching out
The secrets of those flames, which, hidden, waste
A breast made tributary to the laws
Of beauty : physic yet hath never found        40
A remedy to cure a lover's wound.—
Ha ! who are those that cross yon private walk
Into the shadowing grove in amorous foldings ?

    PROPHILUS *passes by, supporting* EUPHRANEA *and*
                *whispering.*

My sister ! O, my sister ! 'tis Euphranea
With Prophilus : supported too ! I would        45

It were an apparition ! Prophilus
Is Ithocles his friend : it strangely puzzles me.

*Re-enter* PROPHILUS *and* EUPHRANEA.

Again ! help me, my book ; this scholar's habit
Must stand my privilege : my mind is busy,
Mine eyes and ears are open.
> [ *Walks aside, pretending to read.*

*Pro.*                    Do not waste          50
The span of this stol'n time, lent by the gods
For precious use, in niceness.   Bright Euphranea,
Should I repeat old vows, or study new,
For purchase of belief to my desires,—

*Org.* [*aside*] Desires !

*Pro.*                    My service, my integrity,—

*Org.* [*aside*] That's better.

*Pro.*                    I should but repeat a lesson
Oft conned without a promptor but thine eyes :
My love is honourable.

*Org.* [*aside*]          So was mine
To my Penthea, chastely honourable.

*Pro.*   Nor wants there more addition to my wish
Of happiness than having thee a wife ;          61
Already sure of Ithocles, a friend
Firm and unalterable.

*Org.* [*aside*]          But a brother
More cruel than the grave.

*Euph.*                    What can you look for,
In answer to your noble protestations,          65
From an unskilful maid, but language suited
To a divided mind ?

*Org.* [*aside*]      Hold out, Euphranea!

*Euph.*   Know, Prophilus, I never undervalued,
From the first time you mentioned worthy love,
Your merit, means, or person : it had been            70
A fault of judgment in me, and a dulness
In my affections, not to weigh and thank
My better stars that offered me the grace
Of so much blissfulness. For, to speak truth,
The law of my desires kept equal pace                75
With yours ; nor have I left that resolution :
But only, in a word, whatever choice
Lives nearest in my heart must first procure
Consent both from my father and my brother,
Ere he can own me his.

*Org.* [*aside*]           She is forsworn else.      80

*Pro.*   Leave me that task.

*Euph.*                   My brother, ere he parted
To Athens, had my oath.

*Org.* [*aside*]             Yes, yes, he had, sure.

*Pro.*   I doubt not, with the means the court sup-
     plies,
But to prevail at pleasure.

*Org.* [*aside*]                 Very likely !

*Pro.*   Meantime, best, dearest, I may build my
     hopes                                           85
On the foundation of thy constant sufferance
In any opposition.

*Euph.*             Death shall sooner
Divorce life and the joys I have in living
Than my chaste vows from truth.

*Pro.*                                    On thy fair hand
I seal the like.

*Org.* [*aside*]   There is no faith in woman.        90
Passion, O, be contained ! my very heart-strings
Are on the tenters.

*Euph.*              We are overheard.
Cupid protect us ! 'twas a stirring, sir,
Of some one near.

*Pro.*          -      Your fears are needless, lady ;
None have access into these private pleasures        95
Except some near in court, or bosom-student
From Tecnicus his oratory, granted
By special favour lately from the king
Unto the grave philosopher.

*Euph.*                    Methinks
I hear one talking to himself,—I see him.        100

*Pro.*   'Tis a poor scholar, as I told you, lady.

*Org.* [*aside*] I am discovered—[*half aloud to him-
self as if studying*] Say it ; is it possible,
With a smooth tongue, a leering countenance,
Flattery, or force of reason—I come t'ye, sir—
To turn or to appease the raging sea ?        105
Answer to that.—Your art ! what art ? to catch
And hold fast in a net the sun's small atoms ?
No, no ; they'll out, they'll out ; ye may as easily
Outrun a cloud driven by a northern blast
As fiddle-faddle so !   Peace, or speak sense.        110

*Euph.*   Call you this thing a scholar ? 'las, he's
lunatic.

*Pro.*   Observe him, sweet ; 'tis but his recreation.

*Org.*  But will you hear a little ? You're so tetchy,
You keep no rule in argument : philosophy
Works not upon impossibilities,                        115
But natural conclusions.—Mew!—absurd!
The metaphysics are but speculations
Of the celestial bodies, or such accidents
As not mixed perfectly, in the air engendered,
Appear to us unnatural ; that's all.                   120
Prove it ; yet, with a reverence to your gravity,
I'll balk illiterate sauciness, submitting
My sole opinion to the touch of writers.

*Pro.*  Now let us fall in with him.

                    [*They come forward.*

*Org.*                          Ha, ha, ha!
These apish boys, when they but taste the gram-
        mates                                          125
And principles of theory, imagine
They can oppose their teachers.   Confidence
Leads many into errors.

*Pro.*                    By your leave, sir.

*Euph.*  Are you a scholar, friend ?

*Org.*                    I am, gay creature,
With pardon of your deities, a mushroom                130
On whom the dew of heaven drops now and then ;
The sun shines on me too, I thank his beams!
Sometime I feel their warmth ; and eat and sleep.

*Pro.*  Does Tecnicus read to thee?

*Org.*                          Yes, forsooth,
He is my master surely ; yonder door                   135
Opens upon his study.

*Pro.* Happy creatures!
Such people toil not, sweet, in heats of state,
Nor sink in thaws of greatness; their affections
Keep order with the limits of their modesty ;
Their love is love of virtue.—What's thy name ?  140

*Org.* Aplotes, sumptuous master, a poor wretch.

*Euph.* Dost thou want anything ?

*Org.* Books, Venus, books.

*Pro.* Lady, a new conceit comes in my thought,
And most available for both our comforts.

*Euph.* My lord,—

*Pro.* Whiles I endeavour to deserve 145
Your father's blessing to our loves, this scholar
May daily at some certain hours attend,
What notice I can write of my success,
Here in this grove, and give it to your hands ;
The like from you to me : so can we never,       150
Barred of our mutual speech, want sure intelligence,
And thus our hearts may talk when our tongues
    cannot.

*Euph.* Occasion is most favourable ; use it.

*Pro.* Aplotes, wilt thou wait us twice a day,
At nine i' the morning and at four at night,       155
Here in this bower, to convey such letters
As each shall send to other ?  Do it willingly,
Safely, and secretly, and I will furnish
Thy study, or what else thou canst desire.

*Org.* Jove, make me thankful, thankful, I beseech
    thee,                                         160

Propitious Jove !   I will prove sure and trusty :
You will not fail me books ?

   *Pro.*                     Nor aught besides
Thy heart can wish.   This lady's name's Euphranea,
Mine Prophilus.

   *Org.*              I have a pretty memory ;
It must prove my best friend.   I will not miss    165
One minute of the hours appointed.

   *Pro.*                          Write
The books thou wouldst have bought thee in a note,
Or take thyself some money.

   *Org.*                     No, no money ;
Money to scholars is a spirit invisible,
We dare not finger it : or books, or nothing.    170

   *Pro.*   Books of what sort thou wilt : do not forget
Our names.

   *Org.*      .   I warrant ye, I warrant ye.

   *Pro.* Smile, Hymen, on the growth of our desires ;
We'll feed thy torches with eternal fires !

          [*Exeunt* PROPHILUS *and* EUPHRANEA.

   *Org.*   Put out thy torches, Hymen, or their light
Shall meet a darkness of eternal night !    176
Inspire me, Mercury, with swift deceits.
Ingenious Fate has leapt into mine arms,
Beyond the compass of my brain.   Mortality
Creeps on the dung of earth, and cannot reach    180
The riddles which are purposed by the gods.
Great arts best write themselves in their own stories ;
They die too basely who outlive their glories. [*Exit.*

# ACT THE SECOND.

## SCENE I. *A Room in* BASSANES' *House.*

### *Enter* BASSANES *and* PHULAS.

*Bass.*   I'll have that window next the street dammed
   up ;
It gives too full a prospect to temptation,
And courts a gazer's glances ; there's a lust
Committed by the eye, that sweats and travails,
Plots, wakes, contrives, till the deformèd bear-whelp,
Adultery, be licked into the act,                          6
The very act : that light shall be dammed up ;
D'ye hear, sir ?

*Phu.*            I do hear, my lord ; a mason
Shall be provided suddenly.

*Bass.*                    Some rogue,
Some rogue of your confederacy,—factor        10
For slaves and strumpets !—to convey close packets
From this spruce springal and the t'other youngster ;
That gaudy earwig, or my lord your patron,
Whose pensioner you are.—I'll tear thy throat out,
Son of a cat, ill-looking hound's head, rip-up        15
Thy ulcerous maw, if I but scent a paper,
A scroll, but half as big as what can cover
A wart upon thy nose, a spot, a pimple,
Directed to my lady ; it may prove
A mystical preparative to lewdness.                  20

*Phu.*   Care shall be had ; I will turn every thread
About me to an eye.—[*Aside*] Here's a sweet life !

*Bass.*   The city housewives, cunning in the traffic
Of chamber merchandise, set all at price
By wholesale ; yet they wipe their mouths and
     simper,                            25
Cull, kiss, and cry "sweetheart," and stroke the head
Which they have branched ; and all is well again !
Dull clods of dirt, who dare not feel the rubs
Stuck on their foreheads.

*Phu.*                      'Tis a villainous world ;
One cannot hold his own in't.

*Bass.*                  Dames at court,   30
Who flaunt in riots, run another bias ;
Their pleasure heaves the patient ass that suffers
Up on the stilts of office, titles, incomes ;
Promotion justifies the shame, and sues for't.
Poor honour, thou art stabbed, and bleed'st to death
By such unlawful hire ! The country mistress   36
Is yet more wary, and in blushes hides
Whatever trespass draws her troth to guilt.
But all are false : on this truth I am bold,
No woman but can fall, and doth, or would.—   40
Now for the newest news about the city ;
What blab the voices, sirrah ?

*Phu.*                  O, my lord,
The rarest, quaintest, strangest, tickling news
That ever—

*Bass.*       Hey-dey ! up and ride me, rascal !
What is't ?

*Phu.*    Forsooth, they say the king has mewed  45

All his gray beard, instead of which is budded
Another of a pure carnation colour,
Speckled with green and russet.

 *Bass.*       Ignorant block!

 *Phu.* Yes, truly ; and 'tis talked about the streets,
That since Lord Ithocles came home, the lions  50
Never left roaring, at which noise the bears
Have danced their very hearts out.

 *Bass.*       Dance out thine too.

 *Phu.* Besides, Lord Orgilus is fled to Athens
Upon a fiery dragon, and 'tis thought
He never can return.

 *Bass.*     Grant it, Apollo!   55

 *Phu.* Moreover, please your lordship, 'tis reported
For certain, that whoever is found jealous
Without apparent proof that's wife is wanton
Shall be divorced : but this is but she-news ;
I had it from a midwife. I have more yet.  60

 *Bass.* Antic, no more ! idiots and stupid fools
Grate my calamities. Why to be fair
Should yield presumption of a faulty soul—
Look to the doors.

 *Phu.*     The horn of plenty crest him !
           [*Aside and exit.*

 *Bass.* Swarms of confusion huddle in my thoughts
In rare distemper.—Beauty ! O, it is   66
An unmatched blessing or a horrid curse.
She comes, she comes ! so shoots the morning forth,
Spangled with pearls of transparent dew.—
The way to poverty is to be rich,    70

As I in her am wealthy ; but for her,
In all contents a bankrupt.

*Enter* PENTHEA *and* GRAUSIS.

Loved Penthea !

How fares my heart's best joy ?

  *Grau.*               In sooth, not well,
She is over-sad.

  *Bass.*        Leave chattering, magpie.—
Thy brother is returned, sweet, safe and honoured
With a triumphant victory ; thou shalt visit him :  76
We will to court, where, if it be thy pleasure,
Thou shalt appear in such a ravishing lustre
Of jewels above value, that the dames
Who brave it there, in rage to be outshined,     80
Shall hide them in their closets, and unseen
Fret in their tears ; whiles every wondering eye
Shall crave none other brightness but thy presence.
Choose thine own recreations ; be a queen
Of what delights thou fanciest best, what company, 85
What place, what times ; do anything, do all things
Youth can command, so thou wilt chase these clouds
From the pure firmament of thy fair looks.

  *Grau.*  Now 'tis well said, my lord.—What, lady !
    laugh,
Be merry ; time is precious.

  *Bass.* [*aside*]          Furies whip thee !  90

  *Pen.*  Alas, my lord, this language to your hand-maid
Sounds as would music to the deaf ; I need
No braveries nor cost of art to draw
The whiteness of my name into offense :

Let such, if any such there are, who covet          95
A curiosity of admiration,
By laying·out their plenty to full view,
Appear in gaudy outsides ; my attires
Shall suit the inward fashion of my mind ;
From which, if your opinion, nobly placed,          100
Change not the livery your words bestow,
My fortunes with my hopes are at the highest.

   *Bass.*   This house, methinks, stands somewhat too
     much inward,
It is too melancholy ; we'll remove
Nearer the court : or what thinks my Penthea          105
Of the delightful island we command ?
Rule me as thou canst wish.

   *Pen.*              I am no mistress :
Whither you please, I must attend ; all ways
Are alike pleasant to me.

   *Grau.*           Island ! prison ;
A prison is as gaysome : we'll no islands ;          110
Marry, out upon 'em ! whom shall we see there ?
Sea-gulls, and porpoises, and water-rats,
And crabs, and mews, and dog-fish ; goodly gear
For a young lady's dealing,—or an old one's !
On no terms islands ; I'll be stewed first.

   *Bass.* [*aside to* GRAUSIS]       Grausis,  115
You are a juggling bawd.—This sadness, sweetest,
Becomes not youthful blood.—[*Aside to* GRAUSIS] I'll
     have you pounded.—
For my sake put on a more cheerful mirth ;
Thou'lt mar thy cheeks, and make me old in griefs.—
[*Aside to* GRAUSIS] Damnable bitch-fox !

*Grau.*                    I am thick of hearing,    120
Still, when the wind blows southerly.—What think ye,
If your fresh lady breed young bones, my lord !
Would not a chopping boy d'ye good at heart ?
But, as you said—

*Bass.* [*aside to* GRAUSIS] I'll spit thee on a stake,
Or chop thee into collops !

*Grau.*                    Pray, speak louder.  125
Sure, sure the wind blows south still.

*Pen.*                    Thou prat'st madly.

*Bass.*  'Tis very hot ; I sweat extremely.


*Re-enter* PHULAS.

                              Now ?

*Phu.*   A herd of lords, sir.

*Bass.*                 Ha !

*Phu.*                    A flock of ladies.

*Bass.*  Where ?

*Phu.*          Shoals of horses.

*Bass.*                    Peasant, how ?

*Phu.*                         Caroches
In drifts ; the one enter, the other stand without, sir :
And now I vanish.                    [*Exit.*


*Enter* PROPHILUS, HEMOPHIL, GRONEAS, CHRISTALLA,
        *and* PHILEMA.

*Pro.*              Noble Bassanes !       131

*Bass.*  Most welcome, Prophilus ; ladies, gentle-
    men,
To all my heart is open ; you all honour me,—

[*Aside*] A tympany swells in my head already.—
Honour me bountifully.—[*Aside*] How they flutter,
Wagtails and jays together!

   *Pro.* From your brother 136
By virtue of your love to him, I require
Your instant presence, fairest.

   *Pen.* He is well, sir?

   *Pro.* The gods preserve him ever! Yet, dear
   beauty,
I find some alteration in him lately, 140
Since his return to Sparta.—My good lord,
I pray, use no delay.

   *Bass.* We had not needed
An invitation, if his sister's health
Had not fall'n into question.—Haste, Penthea,
Slack not a minute.—Lead the way, good Prophilus;
I'll follow, step by step.

   *Pro.* Your arm, fair madam. 146
      [*Exeunt all but* BASSANES *and* GRAUSIS.

   *Bass.* One word with your old bawdship: th'
   hadst been better
Railed at the sins thou worshipp'st than have
   thwarted
My will: I'll use thee cursedly.

   *Grau.* You dote,
You are beside yourself. A politician 150
In jealousy? no, you're too gross, too vulgar.
Pish, teach not me my trade; I know my cue:
My crossing you sinks me into her trust,
By which I shall know all; my trade's a sure one.

*Bass.*   Forgive me, Grausis, 'twas consideration
I relished not; but have a care now.

*Grau.*                          Fear not,    156
I am no new-come-to't.

*Bass.*                Thy life's upon it,
And so is mine.   My agonies are infinite.   [*Exeunt.*

SCENE II.   *The Palace.*   ITHOCLES' *Apartment.*

*Enter* ITHOCLES.

*Ith.*   Ambition! 'tis of vipers' breed : it gnaws
A passage through the womb that gave it motion.
Ambition, like a seelèd dove, mounts upward,
Higher and higher still, to perch on clouds,
But tumbles headlong down with heavier ruins.      5
So squibs and crackers fly into the air,
Then, only breaking with a noise, they vanish
In stench and smoke.   Morality applied
To timely practice, keeps the soul in tune,
At whose sweet music all our actions dance :      10
But this is formed of books and school-tradition ;
It physics not the sickness of a mind
Broken with griefs : strong fevers are not eased
With counsel, but with best receipts and means ;
Means, speedy means and certain ; that's the cure. 15

*Enter* ARMOSTES *and* CROTOLON.

*Arm.*   You stick, Lord Crotolon, upon a point
Too nice and too unnecessary ; Prophilus
Is every way desertful.   I am confident
Your wisdom is too ripe to need instruction
From your son's tutelage.

*Crot.*                    Yet not so ripe,      20
My Lord Armostes, that it dare to dote
Upon the painted meat of smooth persuasion,
Which tempts me to a breach of faith.

*Ith.*                                   Not yet
Resolved, my lord ?  Why, if your son's consent
Be so available, we'll write to Athens      25
For his repair to Sparta : the king's hand
Will join with our desires ; he has been moved to't.

*Arm.*  Yes, and the king himself importuned Crotolon
For a dispatch.

*Crot.*          Kings may command ; their wills
Are laws not to be questioned.

*Ith.*                          By this marriage   30
You knit an union so devout, so hearty,
Between your loves to me and mine to yours,
As if mine own blood had an interest in it ;
For Prophilus is mine, and I am his.

*Crot.*  My lord, my lord!—

*Ith.*            What, good sir ? speak your thought.

*Crot.*  Had this sincerity been real once,      36
My Orgilus had not been now unwived,
Nor your lost sister buried in a bride-bed :
Your uncle here, Amostes, knows this truth ;
For had your father Thrasus lived,—but peace   40
Dwell in his grave! I've done.

*Arm.*                    You're bold and bitter.

*Ith.* [*aside*] He presses home the injury; it
  smarts.—

No reprehensions, uncle ; I deserve 'em,
Yet, gentle sir, consider what the heat
Of an unsteady youth, a giddy brain,               45
Green indiscretion, flattery of greatness,
Rawness of judgment, wilfulness in folly,
Thoughts vagrant as the wind and as uncertain,
Might lead a boy in years to :—'twas a fault,
A capital fault ; for then I could not dive        50
Into the secrets of commanding love ;
Since when experience, by the extremes in others,
Hath forced me collect—and, trust me, Crotolon,
I will redeem those wrongs with any service
Your satisfaction can require for current.         55

  *Arm.*  The acknowledgment is satisfaction :
What would you more ?

  *Crot.*               I'm conquered : if Euphranea
Herself admit the motion, let it be so ;
I doubt not my son's liking.

  *Ith.*                Use my fortunes,
Life, power, sword, and heart,—all are your own.   60

  *Arm.*  The princess, with your sister.

*Enter* CALANTHA, PENTHEA, EUPHRANEA, CHRIS-
    TALLA, PHILEMA, GRAUSIS, BASSANES, *and*
    PROPHILUS.

  *Cal.*                         I present ye
A stranger here in court, my lord ; for did not
Desire of seeing you draw her abroad,
We had not been made happy in her company.

  *Ith.*  You are a gracious princess.—Sister, wedlock
Holds too severe a passion in your nature,         66

Which can engross all duty to your husband,
Without attendance on so dear a mistress.—
[*To* BASSANES] 'Tis not my brother's pleasure, I
    presume,
T'immure her in a chamber.

   *Bass.*                'Tis her will ;     70
She governs her own hours.   Noble Ithocles,
We thank the gods for your success and welfare :
Our lady has of late been indisposed,
Else we had waited on you with the first.

   *Ith.*   How does Penthea now ?

   *Pen.*           You best know, brother, 75
From whom my health and comforts are derived.

   *Bass.* [*aside*] I like the answer well ; 'tis sad and
    modest.
There may be tricks yet, tricks.—Have an eye,
    Grausis !

   *Cal.* Now, Crotolon, the suit we joined in must
    not
Fall by too long demur.

   *Crot.*          'Tis granted, princess,   80
For my part.

   *Arm.*   With condition, that his son
Favour the contract.

   *Cal.*         Such delay is easy.—
The joys of marriage make thee, Prophilus,
A proud deserver of Euphranea's love,
And her of thy desert !

   *Pro.*         Most sweetly gracious !  85

   *Bass.*  The joys of marriage are the heaven on earth,

Life's paradise, great princess, the soul's quiet,
Sinews of concord, earthly immortality,
Eternity of pleasures ;—no restoratives
Like to a constant woman !—[*Aside*] But where is
　　she ?　　　　　　　　　　　　　　　　　　　90
'Twould puzzle all the gods but to create
Such a new monster.—I can speak by proof,
For I rest in Elysium ; 'tis my happiness.

　*Crot.* Euphrànea, how are you resolved, speak
　　freely,
In your affections to this gentleman ?　　　　95

　*Euph.* Nor more nor less than as his love assures
　　me ;
Which—if your liking with my brother's warrants—
I cannot but approve in all points worthy.

　*Crot.* So, so !—[*To* PROPHILUS] I know your
　　answer.

　*Ith.* 　　　　　　　　　　　　'T had been pity
To sunder hearts so equally consented.　　　100

　　　　　　　*Enter* HEMOPHIL.

　*Hem.* The king, Lord Ithocles, commands your
　　presence ;—
And, fairest princess, yours.

　*Cal.* 　　　　　　　　We will attend him.

　　　　　　　*Enter* GRONEAS.

　*Gro.* Where are the lords? all must unto the king
Without delay : the Prince of Argos—

　*Cal.* 　　　　　　　　　　　Well, sir ?

　*Gro.* Is coming to the court, sweet lady.

*Cal.*                                        How  105
The Prince of Argos ?

*Gro.*                    'Twas my fortune, madam,
T' enjoy the honour of these happy tidings.

*Ith.*   Penthea !—

*Pen.*                    Brother ?

*Ith.*                              Let me an hour hence
Meet you alone within the palace-grove ;
I have some secret with you.—Prithee, friend,     110
Conduct her thither, and have special care
The walks be cleared of any to disturb us.

*Pro.* I shall.

*Bass.* [*aside*]   How's that ?

*Ith.*                      Alone, pray be alone.—
I am your creature, princess.—On, my lords !
                    [*Exeunt all but* BASSANES.

*Bass.*   Alone !  alone !  what  means  that  word
    " alone " ?                                115
Why might not I be there ?—hum !—he's her brother.
Brothers and sisters are but flesh and blood,
And this same whoreson court-ease is temptation
To a rebellion in the veins ;—besides,
His fine friend Prophilus must be her guardian :  120
Why may not he dispatch a business nimbly
Before the other come ?—or—pandering, pandering
For one another,—be't to sister, mother,
Wife, cousin, anything,—'mongst youths of mettle
Is in request ; it is so—stubborn fate !        125
But if I be a cuckold, and can know it,
I will be fell, and fell.

*Re-enter* GRONEAS.

*Gro.*                    My lord, you're called for.

*Bass.*   Most heartily I thank ye.   Where's my wife,
   pray?

*Gro.*   Retired amongst the ladies.

*Bass.*                          Still I thank ye.
There's an old waiter with her; saw you her too?

*Gro.*   She sits i' the presence-lobby fast asleep, sir.

*Bass.*   Asleep! asleep, sir!

*Gro.*                    Is your lordship troubled?
You will not to the king?

*Bass.*                    Your humblest vassal.

*Gro.*   Your servant, my good lord.

*Bass.*                          I wait your footsteps.
                                        [*Exeunt.*

SCENE III.   *The Gardens of the Palace.   A Grove.*

*Enter* PROPHILUS *and* PENTHEA.

*Pro.*   In this walk, lady, will your brother find you;
And, with your favour, give me leave a little
To work a preparation.   In his fashion
I have observed of late some kind of slackness
To such alacrity as nature once                            5
And custom took delight in; sadness grows
Upon his recreations, which he hoards
In such a willing silence, that to question
The grounds will argue little skill in friendship,
And less good manners.

*Pen.*                    Sir, I'm not inquisitive   10
Of secrecies without an invitation.

*Pro.*  With pardon, lady, not a syllable
Of mine implies so rude a sense ; the drift—

*Enter* ORGILUS, *disguised as before.*

[*To Org.*]  Do thy best
To make this lady merry for an hour.

    *Org.*  Your will shall be a law, sir.

                    [*Exit* PROPHILUS.

    *Pen.*                Prithee, leave me ;   15
I have some private thoughts I would account with ;
Use thou thine own.

    *Org.*           Speak on, fair nymph ; our souls
Can dance as well to music of the spheres
As any's who have feasted with the gods.

    *Pen.*  Your school-terms are too troublesome.

    *Org.*                 What Heaven
Refines mortality from dross of earth            21
But such as uncompounded beauty hallows
With glorified perfection ?

    *Pen.*            Set thy wits
In a less wild proportion.

    *Org.*           Time can never
On the white table of unguilty faith             25
Write counterfeit dishonour ; turn those eyes,
The arrows of pure love, upon that fire,
Which once rose to a flame, perfumed with vows
As sweetly scented as the incense smoking
On Vesta's altars, . . .                          30
. . . the holiest odours, virgin's tears,
. . . sprinkled, like dews, to feed them
And to increase their fervour.

*Pen.*                              Be not frantic,

*Org.* All pleasures are but mere imagination,
Feeding the hungry appetite with steam                    35
And sight of banquet, whilst the body pines,
Not relishing the real taste of food :
Such is the leanness of a heart divided
From intercourse of troth-contracted loves ;
No horror should deface that precious figure              40
Sealed with the lively stamp of equal souls.

*Pen.* Away ! some Fury hath bewitched thy tongue:
The breath of ignorance, that flies from thence,
Ripens a knowledge in me of afflictions
Above all sufferance.—Thing of talk, begone !            45
Begone, without reply !

*Org.*                    Be just, Penthea,
In thy commands ; when thou send'st forth a doom
Of banishment, know first on whom it lights.
Thus I take off the shroud, in which my cares
Are folded up from view of common eyes.                  50
                  [*Throws off his* Scholar's *dress.*
What is **thy** sentence next ?

*Pen.*                              Rash man ! thou lay'st
A blemish on mine honour, with the hazard
Of thy too-desperate life : yet I profess,
By all the laws of ceremonious wedlock,
I have not given admittance to one thought               55
Of female change since cruelty enforced
Divorce betwixt my body and my heart.
Why would you fall from goodness thus ?

*Org.*                              O, rather
Examine me, how I could live to say

I have been much, much wronged. 'Tis for thy sake
I put on this imposture : dear Penthea,      61
If thy soft bosom be not turned to marble,
Thou'lt pity our calamities ; my interest
Confirms me thou art mine still.

   *Pen.*                     Lend your hand ;
With both of mine I clasp it thus, thus kiss it,    65
Thus kneel before ye.           [PENTHEA *kneels.*

   *Org.*            You instruct my duty.
                    [ORGILUS *kneels.*

   *Pen.* We may stand up. [*They rise.*] Have you
    aught else to urge
Of new demand ? as for the old, forget it ;
'Tis buried in an everlasting silence,
And shall be, shall be ever : what more would ye? 70

   *Org.* I would possess my wife ; the equity
Of very reason bids me.

   *Pen.*              Is that all ?

   *Org.* Why, 'tis the all of me, myself.

   *Pen.*                    Remove
Your steps some distance from me :—at this space
A few words I dare change ; but first put on    75
Your borrowed shape.

   *Org.*          You are obeyed ; 'tis done.
              [*He resumes his disguise.*

   *Pen.* How, Orgilus, by promise I was thine
The heavens do witness ; they can witness too
A rape done on my truth : how I do love thee
Yet, Orgilus, and yet, must best appear    80
In tendering thy freedom ; for I find

The constant preservation of thy merit,
By thy not daring to attempt my fame
With injury of any loose conceit,
Which might give deeper wound to discontents.          85
Continue this fair race : then, though I cannot
Add to thy comfort, yet I shall more often
Remember from what fortune I am fall'n,
And pity mine own ruin.—Live, live happy,—
Happy in thy next choice, that thou mayst people          90
This barren age with virtues in thy issue !
And O, when thou art married, think on me
With mercy, not contempt ! I hope thy wife,
Hearing my story, will not scorn my fall.—
Now let us part.

*Org.*          Part ! yet advise thee better :          95
Penthea is the wife to Orgilus,
And ever shall be.

*Pen.*          Never shall nor will.

*Org.* How !

*Pen.*          Hear me ; in a word I'll tell thee why.
The virgin-dowry which my birth bestowed
Is ravished by another ; my true love          100
Abhors to think that Orgilus deserved
No better favours than a second bed.

*Org.* I must not take this reason.

*Pen.*                    To confirm it ;
Should I outlive my bondage, let me meet
Another worse than this and less desired,          105
If, of all men alive, thou shouldst but touch
My lip or hand again !

*Org.*          Penthea, now

I tell ye, you grow wanton in my sufferance :
Come, sweet, thou'rt mine.

    *Pen.*               Uncivil sir, forbear !
Or I can turn affection into vengeance ;        110
Your reputation, if you value any,
Lies bleeding at my feet.   Unworthy man,
If ever henceforth thou appear in language,
Message, or letter, to betray my frailty,
I'll call thy former protestations lust,         115
And curse my stars for forfeit of my judgment.
Go thou, fit only for disguise, and walks,
To hide thy shame : this once I spare thy life.
I laugh at my own confidence ; my sorrows
By thee are made inferior to my fortunes.      120
If ever thou didst harbour worthy love,
Dare not to answer.   My good genius guide me,
That I may never see thee more !—Go from me !

    *Org.*   I'll tear my veil of politic French off,
And stand up like a man resolved to do :      125
Action, not words, shall show me.—O Penthea!
                                [*Exit.*

    *Pen.*   He sighed my name, sure, as he parted from
       me :
I fear I was too rough.   Alas, poor gentleman !
He looked not like the ruins of his youth,
But like the ruins of those ruins.   Honour,     130
How much we fight with weakness to preserve thee !
                            [*Walks aside.*

    *Enter* BASSANES *and* GRAUSIS.

    *Bass.*   Fie on thee ! damn thee, rotten maggot,
       damn thee !

Sleep? sleep at court? and now? Aches, convulsions,
Imposthumes, rheums, gouts, palsies, clog thy bones
A dozen years more yet!

*Grau.*                    Now you're in humours.   135

*Bass.*   She's by herself, there's hope of that; she's
    sad too;
She's in strong contemplation; yes, and fixed:
The signs are wholesome.

*Grau.*                    Very wholesome, truly.

*Bass.*   Hold your chops, nightmare!—Lady, come;
    your brother
Is carried to his closet; you must thither.          140

*Pen.*   Not well, my lord?

*Bass.*                    A sudden fit; 'twill off!
Some surfeit or disorder.—How dost, dearest?

*Pen.*   Your news is none o' the best.

*Re-enter* PROPHILUS.

*Pro.*                    The chief of men,
The excellentest Ithocles, desires
Your presence, madame.

*Bass.*                    We are hasting to him.

*Pen.*   In vain we labour in this course of life   146
To piece our journey out at length, or crave
Respite of breath: our home is in the grave.

*Bass.*   Perfect philosophy!

*Pen.*                    Then let us care
To live so, that our reckonings may fall even       150
When we're to make account.

*Pro.*                    He cannot fear

Who builds on noble grounds : sickness or pain
Is the deserver's exercise ; and such
Your virtuous brother to the world is known.
Speak comfort to him, lady ; be all gentle :      155
Stars fall but in the grossness of our sight ;
A good man dying, the earth doth lose a light.

                                [*Exeunt.*

# ACT THE THIRD.

## SCENE I. *The Study of* TECNICUS.

*Enter* TECNICUS, *and* ORGILUS *in his usual dress.*

*Tec.*  Be well advised ; let not a resolution
Of giddy rashness choke the breath of reason.

*Org.*  It shall not, most sage master.

*Tec.*                                    I am jealous ;
For if the borrowed shape so late put on
Inferred a consequence, we must conclude          5
Some violent design of sudden nature
Hath shook that shadow off, to fly upon
A new-hatched execution. , Orgilus,
Take heed thou hast not, under our integrity,
Shrouded unlawful plots ; our mortal eyes          10
Pierce not the secrets of your heart, the gods
Are only privy to them.

*Org.*                          Learnèd Tecnicus,
Such doubts are causeless ; and, to clear the truth
From misconceit, the present state commands me.
The Prince of Argos comes himself in person          15
In quest of great Calantha for his bride,
Our kingdom's heir ; besides, mine only sister,
Euphranea, is disposed to Prophilus ;
Lastly, the king is sending letters for me

To Athens, for my quick repair to court :　　20
Please to accept these reasons.

　　*Tec.*　　　　　　　　　Just ones, Orgilus,
Not to be contradicted : yet beware
Of an unsure foundation ; no fair colours
Can fortify a building faintly jointed.
I have observed a growth in thy aspéct　　25
Of dangerous extent, sudden, and—look to't—
I might add, certain—

　　*Org.*　　　　　　　My aspéct ! could art
Run through mine inmost thoughts, it should not sift
An inclination there more than what suited
With justice of mine honour.

　　*Tec.*　　　　　　　　I believe it.　　30
But know then, Orgilus, what honour is :
Honour consists not in a bare opinion
By doing any act that feeds content,
Brave in appearance, 'cause we think it brave ;
Such honour comes by accident, not nature,　　35
Proceeding from the vices of our passion,
Which makes our reason drunk ; but real honour
Is the reward of virtue, and acquired
By justice, or by valour which for basis
Hath justice to uphold it.　He then fails　　40
In honour, who for lucre or revenge
Commits thefts, murders, treasons, and adulteries,
With suchlike, by intrenching on just laws,
Whose sovereignty is best preserved by justice.
Thus, as you see how honour must be grounded　45
On knowledge, not opinion—for opinion
Relies on probability and accident,

But knowledge on necessity and truth,—
I leave thee to the fit consideration
Of what becomes the grace of real honour,          50
Wishing success to all thy virtuous meanings.

   *Org.*   The gods increase thy wisdsm, reverend
     oracle,
And in thy precepts make me ever thrifty !

   *Tec.*   I thank thy wish.          [*Exit* ORGILUS.
                 Much mystery of fate
Lies hid in that man's fortunes ; curiosity          55
May lead his actions into rare attempts :—
But let the gods be moderators still ;
No human power can prevent their will.


       *Enter* ARMOSTES *with a casket.*


From whence come ye ?

   *Arm.*            From King Amyclas,—pardon
My interruption of your studies,—Here,          60
In this sealed box, he sends a treasure to you,
Dear to him as his crown ; he prays your gravity,
You would examine, ponder, sift, and bolt
The pith and circumstance of every tittle
The scroll within contains.

   *Tec.*           What is't, Armostes ? 65

   *Arm.*   It is the health of Sparta, the king's life,
Sinews and safety of the commonwealth ;
The sum of what the oracle delivered
When last he visited the prophetic temple
At Delphos ; what his reasons are, for which,          70
After so long a silence, he requires

Your counsel now, grave man, his majesty
Will soon himself acquaint you with.

   *Tec.*                Apollo [*He takes the casket.*
Inspire my intellect !—The Prince of Argos
Is entertained ?

   *Arm.*         He is ; and has demanded     75
Our princess for his wife ; which I conceive
One special cause the king impórtunes you
For resolution of the oracle.

   *Tec.*   My duty to the king, good peace to Sparta,
And fair day to Armostes !

   *Arm.*            Like to Tecnicus ! [*Exeunt.*


SCENE II.   *The Palace.*  ITHOCLES' *Apartment.*

*Soft music. A song within, during which* PROPHILUS,
BASSANES, PENTHEA, *and* GRAUSIS *pass over the
stage.* BASSANES *and* GRAUSIS *re-enter softly, and
listen in different places.*


SONG.

Can you paint a thought ? or number
Every fancy in a slumber ?
Can you count soft minutes roving
From a dial's point by moving?
Can you grasp a sigh ? or, lastly,      5
Rob a virgin's honour chastely?
  No, O, no ! yet you may
Sooner do both that and this,
This and that, and never miss,
  Than by any praise display      10

Beauty's beauty ; such a glory,
As beyond all fate, all story,
    All arms, all arts,
    All loves, all hearts,
Greater than those or they,   ·          15
  Do, shall, and must obey.

*Bass.* All silent, calm, secure.—Grausis, no
  creaking ?
No noise ? dost thou hear nothing ?

*Grau.*                    Not a mouse,
Or whisper of the wind.

*Bass.*             The floor is matted ;
The bedposts sure are steel or marble.—Soldiers  20
Should not affect, methinks, strains so effeminate :
Sounds of such delicacy are but fawnings
Upon the sloth of luxury, they heighten
Cinders of covert lust up to a flame.

*Grau.* What do you mean, my lord ? speak low ;
  that gabbling                       25
Of yours will but undo us.

*Bass.*             Chamber-combats
Are felt, not heard.

*Pro.* [*within*] He wakes.

*Bass.*             What's that ?

*Ith.* [*within*]             Who's there ?
Sister ?—All quit the room else.

*Bass.*              'Tis consented !

          *Re-enter* PROPHILUS.

*Pro.* Lord Bassanes, your brother would be
  private,

We must forbear ; his sleep hath newly left him.  30
Please ye withdraw.

*Bass.*                    By any means ; 'tis fit.

*Pro.*   Pray, gentlewoman, walk too.

*Grau.*                        Yes, I will, sir. [*Exeunt.*

*The scene opens ;* ITHOCLES *is discovered in a chair, and*
PENTHEA *beside him.*

*Ith.*   Sit nearer, sister, to me ; nearer yet :
We had one father, in one womb took life,
Were brought up twins together, yet have lived    35
At distance, like two strangers : I could wish
That the first pillow whereon I was cradled
Had proved to me a grave.

*Pen.*                        You had been happy :
Then had you never known that sin of life
Which blots all following glories with a vengeance,
For forfeiting the last will of the dead,          41
For whom you had your being.

*Ith.*                        Sad Penthea,
Thou canst not be too cruel ; my rash spleen
Hath with a violent hand plucked from thy bosom
A love-blest heart, to grind it into dust ;        45
For which mine's now a-breaking.

*Pen.*                        Not yet, Heaven,
I do beseech thee ! first let some wild fires
Scorch, not consume it ! may the heat be cherished
With desires infinite, but hopes impossible !

*Ith.* Wronged soul, thy prayers are heard.

*Pen.*                        Here, lo, I breathe,

A miserable creature, led to ruin                    51
By an unnatural brother !

*Ith.*                    I consume
In languishing affections for that trespass ;
Yet cannot die.

*Pen.*                The handmaid to the wages
Of country toil drinks the untroubled streams        55
With leaping kids and with the bleating lambs,
And so allays her thirst secure ; whiles I
Quench my hot sighs with fleetings of my tears.

*Ith.*    The labourer doth eat his coarsest bread,
Earned with his sweat, and lies him down to sleep ;
While every bit I touch turns in digestion           61
To gall as bitter as Penthea's curse.
Put me to any penance for my tyranny,
And I will call thee merciful.

*Pen.*                        Pray kill me,
Rid me from living with a jealous husband ;          65
Then we will join in friendship, be again
Brother and sister.—Kill me, pray ; nay, will ye ?

*Ith.*    How does my lord esteem thee ?

*Pen.*                            Such an one
As only you have made me ; a faith-breaker,
A spotted whore :—forgive me, I am one—              70
In act, not in desires, the gods must witness.

*Ith.*    Thou dost belie thy friend.

*Pen.*                        I do not, Ithocles ;
For she that's wife to Orgilus, and lives
In known adultery with Bassanes,
Is at the best a whore.    Wilt kill me now ?        75

The ashes of our parents will assume
Some dreadful figure, and appear to charge
Thy bloody guilt, that hast betrayed their name
To infamy in this reproachful match.

   *Ith.*   After my victories abroad, at home      80
I meet despair ; ingratitude of nature
Hath made my actions monstrous : thou shalt stand
A deity,. my sister, and be worshipped
For thy resolvèd martyrdom ; wronged maids
And married wives shall to thy hallowed shrine    85
Offer their orisons, and sacrifice
Pure turtles, crowned with myrtle ; if thy pity
Unto a yielding brother's pressure lend
One finger but to ease it.

   *Pen.*               O, no more !

   *Ith.*   Death waits to waft me to the Stygian banks,
And free me from this chaos of my bondage ;    91
And till thou wilt forgive, I must endure.

   *Pen.*   Who is the saint you serve ?

   *Ith.*             Friendship, or nearness
Of birth to any but my sister, durst not
Have moved that question ; 'tis a secret, sister,   95
I dare not murmur to myself.

   *Pen.*             Let me,
By your new protestations I conjure ye,
Partake her name.

   *Ith.*          Her name ?—'tis—'tis—I dare not.

   *Pen.*   All your respects are forged.

   *Ith.*          They are not.—Peace !
Calantha is—the princess—the king's daughter—

Sole heir of Sparta.—Me, most miserable !　　101
Do I now love thee ? for my injuries
Revenge thyself with bravery, and gossip
My treasons to the king's ears, do :—Calantha
Knows it not yet, nor Prophilus, my nearest.　　105

 *Pen.* Suppose you were contracted to her, would it
  not
Split even your very soul to see her father
Snatch her out of your arms against her will,
And force her on the Prince of Argos ?

 *Ith.*         Trouble not
The fountains of mine eyes with thine own story;
I sweat in blood for't.

 *Pen.*      We are reconciled.　　111
Alas, sir, being children but two branches
Of one stock, 'tis not fit we should divide :
Have comfort, you may find it.

 *Ith.*       Yes, in thee ;
Only in thee, Penthea mine.

 *Pen.*      If sorrows　　115
Have not too much dulled my infected brain,
I'll cheer invention for an active strain.

 *Ith.* Mad man ! why have I wronged a maid so
  excellent !

BASSANES *rushes in with a poniard, followed by* PRO-
 PHILUS, GRONEAS, HEMOPHIL, *and* GRAUSIS.

 *Bass.* I can forbear no longer ; more, I will not :
Keep off your hands, or fall upon my point.—　　120
Patience is tired ; for, like a slow-paced ass,

Ye ride my easy nature, and proclaim
My sloth to vengeance a reproach and property.

   *Ith.*   The meaning of this rudeness ?

   *Pro.*                          He's distracted.

   *Pen.*   O, my grieved lord !—

   *Grau.*           Sweet lady, come not near him ;
He holds his perilous weapon in his hand       126
To prick he cares not whom nor where,—see, see,
   see !

   *Bass.*   My birth is noble : though the popular
   blast
Of vanity, as giddy as thy youth,
Hath reared thy name up to bestride a cloud,   130
Or progress in the chariot of the sun,
I am no clod of trade, to lackey pride,
Nor, like your slave of expectation, wait
The bawdy hinges of your doors, or whistle
For mystical conveyance to your bed-sports.   135

   *Gro.*   Fine humours ! they become him.

   *Hem.*                    How he stares,
Struts, puffs, and sweats ! most admirable lunacy !

   *Ith.*   But that I may conceive the spirit of wine
Has took possession of your soberer custom,
I'd say you were unmannerly.

   *Pen.*               Dear brother !—  140

   *Bass.*   Unmannerly !—mew, kitling !—smooth for-
   mality
Is usher to the rankness of the blood,
But impudence bears up the train.   Indeed, sir,
Your fiery mettle, or your springal blaze

Of huge renown, is no sufficient royalty          145
To print upon my forehead the scorn, " cuckold."

*Ith.*   His jealousy has robbed him of his wits ;
He talks he knows not what.

*Bass.*                         Yes, and he knows
To whom he talks ; to one that franks his lust
In swine-security of bestial incest.              150

*Ith.*  Ha, devil !

*Bass.*          I will halloo't ; though I blush more
To name the filthiness than thou to act it.

*Ith.*  Monster !          [*Draws his sword.*

*Pro.*          Sir, by our friendship—

*Pen.*                    By our bloods—
Will you quite both undo us, brother ?

*Grau.*                    Out on him !
These are his megrims, firks, and melancholies.   155

*Hem.*  Well said, old touch-hole.

*Gro.*                    Kick him out of doors.

*Pen.*  With favour, let me speak.—My lord, what
            slackness
In my obedience hath deserved this rage ?
Except humility and silent duty
Have drawn on your unquiet, my simplicity         160
Ne'er studied your vexation.

*Bass.*                    Light of beauty,
Deal not ungently with a desperate wound !
No breach of reason dares make war with her
Whose looks are sovereignity, whose breath is balm :
O, that I could preserve thee in fruition         165
As in devotion !

*Pen.*                    Sir, may every evil
Locked in Pandora's box shower in your presence
On my unhappy head, if, since you made me
A partner in your bed, I have been faulty
In one unseemly thought against your honour !    170

*Ith.*   Purge not his griefs, Penthea.

*Bass.*                                Yes, say on,
Excellent creature !—[*To* ITHOCLES]   Good, be not
   a hindrance
To peace and praise of virtue.—O, my senses
Are charmed with sounds celestial !—On, dear, on :
I never gave you one ill word ; say, did I ?        175
Indeed I did not.

*Pen.*              Nor, by Juno's forehead,
Was I e'er guilty of a wanton error.

*Bass.*   A goddess ! let me kneel.

*Grau.*                           Alas, kind animal !

*Ith.*   No ; but for penance.

*Bass.*                        Noble sir, what is it ?
With gladness I embrace it ; yet, pray let not      180
My rashness teach you to be too unmerciful.

*Ith.*   When you shall show good proof that manly
   wisdom,
Not overswayed by passion or opinion,
Knows how to lead your judgment, then this lady,
Your wife, my sister, shall return in safety        185
Home, to be guided by you ; but, till first
I can out of clear evidence approve it,
She shall be my care.

*Bass.*              Rip my bosom up,

I'll stand the execution with a constancy ;
This torture is insufferable.

   *Ith.*               Well, sir,        190
I dare not trust her to your fury.

   *Bass.*             But
Penthea says not so.

   *Pen.*       She needs no tongue
To plead excuse who never purposed wrong.
        [*Exit with* ITHOCLES *and* PROPHILUS.

   *Hem.*   Virgin of reverence and antiquity,
Stay you behind.
     [*To* GRAUSIS, *who is following* PENTHEA.

   *Gro.*    The court wants not your diligence.  195
        [*Exeunt* HEMOPHIL *and* GRONEAS.

   *Grau.*   What will you do, my lord ? my lady's gone ;
I am denied to follow.

   *Bass.*          I may see her,
Or speak to her once more ?

   *Grau.*         And feel her too, man ;
Be of good cheer, she's your own flesh and bone.

   *Bass.*   Diseases desperate must find cures alike.
She swore she has been true.

   *Grau.*        True, on my modesty.  201

   *Bass.*   Let him want truth who credits not her
     vows !
Much wrong I did her, but her brother infinite ;
Rumour will voice me the contempt of manhood,
Should I run on thus : some way I must try    205
To outdo art, and jealousy decry.      [*Exeunt.*

SCENE III. *A Room in the Palace.*

*Flourish. Enter* AMYCLAS, NEARCHUS, *leading* CAL-
ANTHA, ARMOSTES, CROTOLON, EUPHRANEA,
CHRISTALLA, PHILEMA, *and* AMELUS.

*Amy.* Cousin of Argos, what the heavens have
    pleased,
In their unchanging counsels, to conclude
For both our kingdoms' weal, we must submit to :
Nor can we be unthankful to their bounties,
Who, when we were even creeping to our grave,    5
Sent us a daughter, in whose birth our hope
Continues of succession. As you are
In title next, being grandchild to our aunt,
So we in heart desire you may sit nearest
Calantha's love ; since we have ever vowed    10
Not to enforce affection by our will,
But by her own choice to confirm it gladly.

*Near.* You speak the nature of a right just father.
I come not hither roughly to demand
My cousin's thraldom, but to free mine own :    15
Report of great Calantha's beauty, virtue,
Sweetness, and singular perfections, courted
All ears to credit what I find was published
By constant truth ; from which, if any service
Of my desert can purchase fair construction,    20
This lady must command it.

*Cal.*                    Princely sir,
So well you know how to profess observance,
That you instruct your hearers to become

Practitioners in duty ; of which number
I'll study to be chief.

*Near.*                     Chief, glorious virgin,          25
In my devotion, as in all men's wonder.

*Amy.*  Excellent cousin, we deny no liberty ;
Use thine own opportunities.—Armostes,
We must consult with the philosophers ;
The business is of weight.

*Arm.*                     Sir, at your pleasure.   30

*Amy.*  You told me, Crotolon, your son's returned
From Athens : wherefore comes he not to court,
As we commanded ?

*Crot.*                     He shall soon attend
Your royal will, great sir.

*Amy.*                     The marriage
Between young Prophilus and Euphranea                35
Tastes of too much delay.

*Crot.*                     My lord,—

*Amy.*                     Some pleasures
At celebration of it would give life
To the entertainment of the prince our kinsman ;
Our court wears gravity more than we relish.

*Arm.*  Yet the heavens smile on all your high
    attempts,                                              40
Without a cloud.

*Crot.*                     So may the gods protect us !

*Cal.*  A prince a subject ?

*Near.*                     Yes, to beauty's sceptre ;
As all hearts kneel, so mine.

*Cal.*                     You are too courtly.

*Enter* ITHOCLES, ORGILUS *and* PROPHILUS.

*Ith.*  Your safe return to Sparta is most welcome :
I joy to meet you here, and, as occasion          45
Shall grant us privacy, will yield you reasons
Why I should covet to deserve the title
Of your respected friend ; for, without compliment,
Believe it, Orgilus, 'tis my ambition.

   *Org.*  Your lordship may command me, your poor
   servant.          50

   *Ith.* [*aside*]  So amorously close !—so soon ! my
   heart !

   *Pro.*  What sudden change is next ?

   *Ith.*                                   Life to the king !
To whom I here present this noble gentleman,
New come from Athens : royal sir, vouchsafe
Your gracious hand in favour of his merit.          55
       [*The* King *gives* ORGILUS *his hand to kiss.*

   *Crot.* [*aside*]  My son preferred by Ithocles !

   *Amy.*                                   Our bounties
Shall open to thee, Orgilus ; for instance,—
Hark in thine ear,—if, out of those inventions
Which flow in Athens, thou hast there engrossed
Some rarity of wit, to grace the nuptials          60
Of thy fair sister, and renown our court
In the eyes of this young prince, we shall be debtor
To thy conceit : think on't.

   *Org.*                                   Your highness honours me.

   *Near.*  My tongue and heart are twins.

   *Cal.*                                   A noble birth,

Becoming such a father.—Worthy Orgilus,          65
You are a guest most wished for.

*Org.*                    May my duty
Still rise in your opinion, sacred princess !

*Ith.*   Euphranea's brother, sir ; a gentleman
Well worthy of your knowledge.

*Near.*                    We embrace him,
Proud of so dear acquaintance.

*Amy.*                    All prepare          70
For revels and disport ; the joys of Hymen,
Like Phœbus in his lustre, put to flight
All mists of dulness, crown the hours with gladness :
No sounds but music, no discourse but mirth !

*Cal.*   Thine arm, I prithee, Ithocles.—Nay, good
My lord, keep on your way ; I am provided.          76

*Near.*   I dare not disobey.

*Ith.*                    Most heavenly lady !
                              [*Exeunt.*


SCENE IV.   *A Room in the House of* CROTOLON.

*Enter* CROTOLON *and* ORGILUS.

*Crot.*   The king hath spoke his mind.

*Org.*                    His will he hath ;
But were it lawful to hold plea against
The power of greatness, not the reason, haply
Such undershrubs as subjects sometimes might
Borrow of nature justice, to inform          5
The license sovereignty holds without check
Over a meek obedience.

*Crot.*                    How resolve you

Touching your sister's marriage ?   Prophilus
Is a deserving and a hopeful youth.

*Org.*   I envy not his merit, but applaud it ;      10
Could wish him thrift in all his best desires,
And with a willingness inleague our blood
With his, for purchase of full growth in friendship,
He never touched on any wrong that maliced
The honour of our house nor stirred our peace :     15
Yet, with your favour, let me not forget
Under whose wing he gathers warmth and comfort,
Whose creature he is bound, made, and must live so.

*Crot.*   Son, son, I find in thee a harsh condition ;
No courtesy can win it, 'tis too rancorous.          20

*Org.*   Good sir, be not severe in your construction ;
I am no stranger to such easy calms
As sit in tender bosoms : lordly Ithocles
Hath graced my entertainment in abundance ;
Too humbly hath descended from that height      25
Of arrogance and spleen which wrought the rape
On grieved Penthea's purity ; his scorn
Of my untoward fortunes is reclaimed
Unto a courtship, almost to a fawning :—
I'll kiss his foot, since you will have it so.          30

*Crot.*   Since I will have it so ! friend, I will have
   it so,
Without our ruin by your politic plots,
Or wolf of hatred snarling in your breast.
You have a spirit, sir, have ye ? a familiar
That posts i' the air for your intelligence ?          35
Some such hobgoblin hurried you from Athens,
For yet you come unsent for.

*Org.*                          If unwelcome,
I might have found a grave there.

   *Crot.*                          Sure, your business
Was soon dispatched, or your mind altered quickly.

   *Org.*   'Twas care, sir, of my health cut short my
        journey ;                                        40
For there a general infection
Threatens a desolation.

   *Crot.*                 And I fear
Thou hast brought back a worse infection with thee,—
Infection of thy mind ; which, as thou say'st,
Threatens the desolation of our family.              45

   *Org.*   Forbid it, our dear genius ! I will rather
Be made a sacrifice on Thrasus' monument,
Or kneel to Ithocles his son in dust,
Than woo a father's curse.   My sister's marriage
With Prophilus is from my heart confirmed ;        50
May I live hated, may I die despised,
If I omit to further it in all
That can concern me !

   *Crot.*                 I have been too rough.
My duty to my king made me so earnest ;
Excuse it, Orgilus.

   *Org.*           Dear sir !—

   *Crot.*                          Here comes        55
Euphranea, with Prophilus and Ithocles.

*Enter* PROPHILUS, EUPHRANEA, ITHOCLES, GRONEAS,
               *and* HEMOPHIL.

   *Org.*   Most honoured !—ever famous !

   *Ith.*                          Your true friend ;

On earth not any truer.—With smooth eyes
Look on this worthy couple ; your consent
Can only make them one.

*Org.*               They have it.—Sister,  60
Thou pawnedst to me an oath, of which engagement
I never will release thee, if thou aim'st
At any other choice than this.

*Euph.*               Dear brother,
At him, or none.

*Crot.*       To which my blessing's added.

*Org.*  Which, till a greater ceremony perfect,—  65
Euphranea, lend thy hand,—here, take her, Prophilus :
Live long a happy man and wife ; and further,
That these in presence may conclude an omen.
Thus for a bridal song I close my wishes :

> [*Sings*]  Comforts lasting, loves increasing,     70
>         Like soft hours never ceasing :
>         Plenty's pleasure, peace complying,
>         Without jars, or tongues envying ;
>         Hearts by holy union wedded,
>         More than theirs by custom bedded ;
>         Fruitful issues ; life so graced,     76
>         Not by age to be defaced,
>         Budding, as the year ensu'th,
>         Every spring another youth :
>         All what thought can add beside     80
>         Crown this bridegroom and this bride !

*Pro.*  You have sealed joy close to my soul.—
    Euphranea,
Now I may call thee mine.

*Ith.*				I but exchange
One good friend for another.

*Org.*				If these gallants
Will please to grace a poor invention				85
By joining with me in some slight device,
I'll venture on a strain my younger days
Have studied for delight.

*Hem.*			With thankful willingness
I offer my attendance.

*Gro.*			No endeavour
Of mine shall fail to show itself.

*Ith.*				We will			90
All join to wait on thy directions, Orgilus.

*Org.* O, my good lord, your favours flow towards
A too unworthy worm ;—but as you please ;
I am what you will shape me.

*Ith.*				A fast friend.

*Crot.* I thank thee, son, for this acknowledgment ;
It is a sight of gladness.

*Org.*				But my duty.	[*Exeunt.*


SCENE V.  CALANTHA'S *Apartment in the Palace.*

*Enter* CALANTHA, PENTHEA, CHRISTALLA, *and*
PHILEMA.

*Cal.* Whoe'er would speak with us, deny his
	entrance ;
Be careful of our charge.

*Chris.*			We shall, madam.

*Cal.*  Except the king  himself, give none admittance ;
Not any.

   *Phil.*   Madam, it shall be our care.
                  [*Exeunt* CHRISTALLA *and* PHILEMA.

   *Cal.*  Being alone, Penthea, you have granted    5
The opportunity you sought, and might
At all times have commanded.

   *Pen.*                  'Tis a benefit
Which I shall owe your goodness even in death for :
My glass of life, sweet princess, hath few minutes
Remaining to run down ; the sands are spent ;    10
For by an inward messenger I feel
The summons of departure short and certain.

   *Cal.*  You feel too much your melancholy.

   *Pen.*                   Glories
Of human greatness are but pleasing dreams
And shadows soon decaying : on the stage    15
Of my mortality my youth hath acted
Some scenes of vanity, drawn out at length
By varied pleasures, sweetened in the mixture,
But tragical in issue : beauty, pomp,
With every sensuality our giddiness    20
Doth frame an idol, are unconstant friends,
When any troubled passion makes assault
On the unguarded castle of the mind.

   *Cal.*  Contemn not your condition for the proof
Of bare opinion only : to what end    25
Reach all these moral texts ?

   *Pen.*               To place before ye
A perfect mirror, wherein you may see

How weary I am of a lingering life,
Who count the best a misery.

   *Cal.*                Indeed
You have no little cause ; yet none so great     30
As to distrust a remedy.

   *Pen.*            That remedy
Must be a winding-sheet, a fold of lead,
And some untrod-on corner in the earth.—
Not to detain your expectation, princess,
I have an humble suit.

   *Cal.*           Speak ; I enjoy it.     35

   *Pen.*   Vouchsafe, then, to be my executrix,
And take that trouble on ye to dispose
Such legacies as I beqeath impartially ;
I have not much to give, the pains are easy ;
Heaven will reward your piety, and thank it     40
When I am dead ; for sure I must not live ;
I hope I cannot.

   *Cal.*         Now, beshrew thy sadness,
Thou turn'st me too much woman.       [*Weeps.*

   *Pen.* [*aside*]          Her fair eyes
Melt into passion.—Then I have assurance
Encouraging my boldness. ·In this paper     45
My will was charactered ; which you, with pardon,
Shall now know from mine own mouth.

   *Cal.*              Talk on, prithee ;
It is a pretty earnest.

   *Pen.*         I have left me
But three poor jewels to bequeath. The first is
My youth ; for though I am much old in griefs,    50
In years I am a child.

*Cal.* To whom that jewel?

*Pen.* To virgin-wives, such as abuse not wedlock
By freedom of desires, but covet chiefly
The pledges of chaste beds for ties of love,
Rather than ranging of their blood ; and next       55
To married maids, such as prefer the number
Of honourable issue in their virtues
Before the flattery of delights by marriage :
May those be ever young !

*Cal.* A second jewel
You mean to part with ?

*Pen.* 'Tis my fame, I trust       60
By scandal yet untouched : this I bequeath
To Memory, and Time's old daughter, Truth.
If ever my unhappy name find mention
When I am fall'n to dust, may it deserve
Beseeming charity without dishonour !       65

*Cal.* How handsomely thou play'st with harmless
     sport
Of mere imagination ! speak the last.
I strangely like thy will.

*Pen.* This jewel, madam,
Is dearly precious to me ; you must use
The best of your discretion to employ       70
This gift as I intend it.

*Cal.* Do not doubt me.

*Pen.* 'Tis long agone since first I lost my heart :
Long I have lived without it, else for certain
I should have given that too ; but instead
Of it, to great Calantha, Sparta's heir,       75

By service bound and by affection vowed,
I do bequeath, in holest rites of love,
Mine only brother, Ithocles.

 *Cal.*      What saidst thou?

 *Pen.* Impute not, heaven-blest lady, to ambition
A faith as humbly perfect as the prayers    80
Of a devoted suppliant can endow it:
Look on him, princess, with an eye of pity;
How like the ghost of what he late appeared
He moves before you.

 *Cal.*     Shall I answer here,
Or lend my ear too grossly?

 *Pen.*      First his heart  85
Shall fall in cinders, scorched by your disdain,
Ere he will dare, poor man, to ope an eye
On these divine looks, but with low-bent thoughts
Accusing such presumption; as for words,
He dares not utter any but of service:    90
Yet this lost creature loves ye.—Be a princess
In sweetness as in blood; give him his doom,
Or raise him up to comfort.

 *Cal.*     What new change
Appears in my behaviour, that thou dar'st
Tempt my displeasure?

 *Pen.*     I must leave the world 95
To revel in Elysium, and 'tis just
To wish my brother some advantage here;
Yet, by my best hopes, Ithocles is ignorant
Of this pursuit: but if you please to kill him,
Lend him one angry look or one harsh word,  100
And you shall soon conclude how strong a power

Your absolute authority holds over
His life and end.

    *Cal.*             You have forgot, Penthea,
How still I have a father.

    *Pen.*                But remember
I am a sister, though to me this brother        105
Hath been, you know, unkind, O, most unkind !

    *Cal.*   Christalla, Philema, where are ye ?—Lady,
Your check lies in my silence.

*Re-enter* Christalla *and* Philema.

*Chris. and Phil.*             Madam, here.

    *Cal.*   I think ye sleep, ye drones : wait on Penthea
Unto her lodging.—[*Aside*] Ithocles ? wronged lady !

    *Pen.*   My reckonings are made even ; death or
        fate                            III
Can now nor strike too soon nor force too late.

[*Exeunt.*

# ACT THE FOURTH.

SCENE I. *The Palace.* ITHOCLES' *Apartment.*

*Enter* ITHOCLES *and* ARMOSTES.

*Ith.*   Forbear your inquisition ; curiosity
Is of too subtle and too searching nature,
In fears of love too quick, too slow of credit.—
I am not what you doubt me.

*Arm.*                              Nephew, be, then,
As I would wish ;—all is not right.—Good heaven   5
Confirm your resolutions for dependence
On worthy ends, which may advance your quiet !

*Ith.*   I did the noble Orgilus much injury,
But grieved Penthea more : I now repent it,—
Now, uncle, now ; this " now " is now too late.      10
So provident is folly in sad issue,
That after-wit, like bankrupts' debts, stands tallied,
Without all possibilities of payment.
Sure, he's an honest, very honest gentleman ;
A man of single meaning.

*Arm.*                         I believe it :          15
Yet, nephew, 'tis the tongue informs our ears ;
Our eyes can never pierce into the thoughts,
For they are lodged too inward :—but I question
No truth in Orgilus.—The princess, sir.

*Ith.* The princess ! ha !

*Arm.*  With her the Prince of Argos.  20

*Enter* Nearchus, *leading* Calantha ; Amelus, Christalla, Philema.

*Near.* - Great fair one, grace my hopes with any instance
Of livery, from the allowance of your favour ;
This little spark—
  [*Attempts to take a ring from her finger.*

*Cal.*  A toy !

*Near.*  Love feasts on toys,
For Cupid is a child ;—vouchsafe this bounty :
It cannot be denied.

*Cal.*  You shall not value,  25
Sweet cousin, at a price, what I count cheap ;
So cheap, that let him take it who dares stoop for't,
And give it at next meeting to a mistress :
She'll thank him for't, perhaps.
  [*Casts the ring before* Ithocles, *who takes it up.*

*Ame.*  The ring, sir, is
The princess's ; I could have took it up.  30

*Ith.* Learn manners, prithee.—To the blessèd owner,
Upon my knees—  [*Kneels and offers it to* Calantha.

*Near.*  You're saucy.

*Cal.*  This is pretty !
I am, belike, " a mistress "—wondrous pretty !—

Let the man keep his fortune, since he found it ;
He's worthy on't.—On, cousin !

> [*Exeunt* NEARCHUS, CALANTHA, CHRIS-
> TALLA, *and* PHILEMA.

*Ith.* [*to* AMELUS]　　　　　　Follow, spaniel ;　35
I'll force ye to a fawning else.

*Ame.*　　　　　　　　　You dare not.　[*Exit.*

*Arm.*　My lord, you were too forward.

*Ith.*　　　　　　　　　Look ye, uncle,
Some such there are whose liberal contents
Swarm without care in every sort of plenty ;
Who after full repasts can lay them down　　　40
To sleep ; and they sleep, uncle : in which silence
Their very dreams present 'em choice of pleasures,
Pleasures—observe me, uncle—of rare object ;
Here heaps of gold, there increments of honours,
Now change of garments, then the votes of people ;
Anon varieties of beauties, courting,　　　　46
In flatteries of the night, exchange of dalliance :
Yet these are still but dreams.　Give me felicity
Of which my senses waking are partakers,
A real, visible, material happiness ;　　　　50
And then, too, when I stagger in expectance
Of the least comfort that can cherish life.—
I saw it sir, I saw it ! for it came
From her own hand.

*Arm.*　　　　　　The princess threw it t'ye.

*Ith.*　True ; and she said—well I remember what—
Her cousin prince would beg it.

*Arm.*　　　　　　　　Yes, and parted　56
In anger at your taking on't.

*Ith.*                         Penthea,
O, thou hast pleaded with a powerful language!
I want a fee to gratify thy merit ;
But I will do—

*Arm.*          What is't you say?

*Ith.*                              In anger !  60
In anger let him part ; for could his breath,
Like whirlwinds, toss such servile slaves as lick
The dust his footsteps print into a vapour,
It durst not stir a hair of mine, it should not ;
I'd rend it up by the roots first.   To be anything  65
Calantha smiles on, is to be a blessing
More sacred than a petty prince of Argos
Can wish to equal or in worth or title.

*Arm.*   Contain yourself, my lord : Ixion, aiming
To embrace Juno, bosomed but a cloud,            70
And begat Centaurs ; 'tis an useful moral :
Ambition hatched in clouds of mere opinion
Proves but in birth a prodigy.

*Ith.*                         I thank ye ;
Yet, with your license, I should seem uncharitable
To gentler fate, if, relishing the dainties      75
Of a soul's settled peace, I were so feeble
Not to digest it.

*Arm.*          He deserves small trust
Who is not privy-counsellor to himself.

*Re-enter* NEARCHUS *and* AMELUS, *with* ORGILUS.

*Near.*   Brave me?

*Org.*          Your excellence mistakes his temper ;
For Ithocles in fashion of his mind            80

Is beautiful, soft, gentle, the clear mirror
Of absolute perfection

*Ame.*                  Was't your modesty
Termed any of the prince's servants " spaniel " ?
Your nurse, sure, taught you other language.

*Ith.*                                   Language !

*Near.*   A gallant man-at-arms is here, a doctor   85
In feats of chivalry, blunt and rough-spoken,
Vouchsafing not the fustian of civility,
Which less rash spirits style good manners.

*Ith.*                                   Manners !

*Org.*   No  more,  illustrious  sir ;  'tis  matchless
      Ithocles.

*Near.*   You might have understood who I am.

*Ith.*                                   Yes,   90
I did ; else—but the presence calmed the affront—
You're cousin to the princess.

*Near.*                   To the king too ;
A certain instrument that lent supportance
To your colossic greatness—to that king too,
You might have added.

*Ith.*                   There is more divinity   95
In beauty than in majesty.

*Arm.*                   O fie, fie !

*Near.*   This odd youth's pride turns heretic in
      loyalty.
Sirrah ! low mushrooms never rival cedars.

                   [*Exeunt* NEARCHUS *and* AMELUS.

*Ith.*   Come back !—What pitiful dull thing am I

So to be tamely scolded at ! come back !—           100
Let him come back, and echo once again
That scornful sound of mushroom ! painted colts—
Like heralds' coats gilt o'er with crowns and sceptres—
May bait a muzzled lion.

   *Arm.*              Cousin, cousin,
Thy tongue is not thy friend.

   *Org.*           In point of honour   105
Discretion knows no bounds.   Amelus told me
'Twas all about a little ring.

   *Ith.*             A ring
The princess threw away, and I took up :
Admit she threw't to me, what arm of brass
Can snatch it hence ?   No ; could he grind the hoop
To powder, he might sooner reach my heart       111
Than steal and wear one dust on't.—Orgilus,
I am extremely wronged.

   *Org.*         A lady's favour
Is not to be so slighted.

   *Ith.*        Slighted !

   *Arm.*          Quiet
These vain unruly passions, which will render ye   115
Into a madness.

   *Org.*      Griefs will have their vent.

   *Enter* TECNICUS *with a scroll.*

   *Arm.*  Welcome ; thou com'st in season, reverend
    man,
To pour the balsam of a suppling patience
Into the festering wound of ill-spent fury.

*Org.* [*aside*] What makes he here?

*Tec.*                 The hurts are yet but mortal,
Which shortly will prove deadly.   To the king,   121
Armostes, see in safety thou deliver
This sealed-up counsel ; bid him with a constancy
Peruse the secrets of the gods.—O Sparta,
O Lacedæmon ! double-named, but one        125
In fate : when  kingdoms reel,—mark well my saw,—
Their heads must needs be giddy.   Tell the king
That henceforth he no more must inquire after
My agèd head ; Apollo wills it so :
I am for Delphos.

*Arm.*             Not without some conference   130
With our great master ?

*Tec.*                 Never more to see him :
A greater prince commands me.—Ithocles,
  " When youth is ripe, and age from time doth part,
    The lifeless trunk shall wed the broken heart."

*Ith.*   What's this, if understood ?

*Tec.*                     List, Orgilus ;   135
Remember what I told thee long before,
These tears shall be my witness.

*Arm.*                     'Las, good man !

*Tec.*   " Let craft with courtesy a while confer,
          Revenge proves its own executioner."

*Org.*   Dark  sentences  are  for  Apollo's  priests ;
I am not Œdipus.

*Tec.*                 My hour is come ;        141
Cheer up the king ; farewell to all.—O Sparta,
O Lacedæmon !                      [*Exit.*

*Arm.*           If prophetic fire
Have warmed this old man's bosom, we might construe
His words to fatal sense.

*Ith.*           Leave to the powers   145
Above us the effects of their decrees ;
My burthen lies within me : servile fears
Prevent no great effects.—Divine Calantha !

*Arm.*   The gods be still propitious !
                  [*Exeunt* ITHOCLES *and* ARMOSTES.

*Org.*           Something oddly
The book-man prated, yet he talked it weeping   150
     " Let craft with courtesy a while confer,
       Revenge proves its own executioner."
Con it again ;—for what ?   It shall not puzzle me ;
'Tis dotage of a withered brain.—Penthea
Forbade me not her presence ; I may see her,   155
And gaze my fill.   Why see her, then, I may,
When, if I faint to speak—I must be silent.     [*Exit.*


SCENE II.   *A Room in* BASSANES' *House.*

*Enter* BASSANES, GRAUSIS, *and* PHULAS.

*Bass.*   Pray, use your recreations, all the service
I will expect is quietness amongst ye ;
Take liberty at home, abroad, at all times,
And in your charities appease the gods,
Whom I, with my distractions, have offended.      5

*Grau.*   Fair blessings on thy heart !

*Phu.* [*aside*]          Here's a rare change !
My lord, to cure the itch, is surely gelded ;
The cuckold in conceit hath cast his horns.

*Bass.*  Betake ye to your several occasions ;
And wherein I have heretofore been faulty,          10
Let your constructions mildly pass it over ;
Henceforth I'll study reformation,—more
I have not for employment.

   *Grau.*                      O, sweet man !
Thou art the very " Honeycomb of Honesty."

   *Phu.*  The " Garland of Good-will."—Old lady,
     hold up                                        15
Thy reverend snout, and trot behind me softly,
As it becomes a moil of ancient carriage.

                      [*Exeunt* Grausis *and* Phulas.

   *Bass.*  Beasts, only capable of sense, enjoy
The benefit of food and ease with thankfulness ;
Such silly creatures, with a grudging, kick not          20
Against the portion nature hath bestowed :
But men, endowed with reason and the use
Of reason, to distinguish from the chaff
Of abject scarcity the quintessence,
Soul, and elixir of the earth's abundance,          25
The treasures of the sea, the air, nay, heaven,
Repining at these glories of creation
Are verier beasts than beasts ; and of those beasts
The worst am I : I, who was made a monarch
Of what a heart could wish for,—a chaste wife,—          30
Endeavoured what in me lay to pull down
That temple built for adoration only,
And level't in the dust of causeless scandal.
But, to redeem a sacrilege so impious,
Humility shall pour, before the deities          35
I have incensed, a largess of more patience

Than their displeasèd altars can require :
No tempests of commotion shall disquiet
The calms of my composure.

*Enter* ORGILUS.

*Org.*                    I have found thee,
Thou patron of more horrors than the bulk          40
Of manhood, hooped about with ribs of iron,
Can cram within thy breast ; Penthea, Bassanes,
Cursed by jealousies,—more, by the dotage,—
Is left a prey to words.

*Bass.*                    Exercise
Your trials for addition to my penance ;          45
I am resolved.

*Org.*          Play not with misery
Past cure : some angry minister of fate hath
Deposed the empress of her soul, her reason,
From its most proper throne ; but, what's the miracle
More new, I, I have seen it, and yet live !          50

*Bass.*  You may delude my senses, not my judg-
    ment ;
'Tis anchored into a firm resolution ;
Dalliance of mirth or wit can ne'er unfix it :
Practice yet further.

*Org.*          May thy death of love to her
Damn all thy comforts to a lasting fast          55
From every joy of life !   Thou barren rock,
By thee we have been split in ken of harbour.

*Enter* PENTHEA *with her hair loose,* ITHOCLES,
    ARMOSTES, PHILEMA, *and* CHRISTALLA.

*Ith.*  Sister, look up ; your Ithocles, your brother,

Speaks t'ye ; why do you weep ? dear, turn not from
    me.—
Here is a killing sight ; lo, Bassanes,        60
A lamentable object !

  *Org.*             Man, does see't ?
Sports are more gamesome ; am I yet in merriment ?
Why dost not laugh ?

  *Bass.*          Divine and best of ladies,
Please to forget my outrage ; mercy ever
Cannot but lodge under a roof so excellent :    65
I have cast off that cruelty of frenzy
Which once appeared imposture, and then juggled
To cheat my sleeps of rest.

  *Org.*            Was I in earnest ?

  *Pen.*  Sure, if we were all Sirens, we should sing
    pitifully,
And 'twere a comely music, when in parts    70
One sung another's knell : the turtle sighs
When he hath lost his mate ; and yet some say
He must be dead first : 'tis a fine deceit
To pass away in a dream ! indeed, I've slept
With mine eyes open a great while.   No falsehood
Equals a broken faith ; there's not a hair    76
Sticks on my head but, like a leaden plummet,
It sinks me to the grave : I must creep thither ;
The journey is not long.

  *Ith.*          But thou, Penthea,
Hast many years, I hope, to number yet,    80
Ere thou canst travel that way.

  *Bass.*         Let the sun first
Be wrapped up in an everlasting darkness,

Before the light of nature, chiefly formed
For the whole world's delight, feel an eclipse
So universal !

*Org.*          Wisdom, look ye, begins          85
To rave !—art thou mad too, antiquity ?

*Pen.*   Since I was first a wife, I might have been
Mother to many pretty prattling babes ;
They would have smiled when I smiled, and for certain
I should have cried when they cried :—truly, brother,
My father would have picked me out a husband,   91
And then my little ones had been no bastards ;
But 'tis too late for me to marry now,
I am past child-bearing ; 'tis not my fault.

*Bass.*   Fall on me, if there be a burning Ætna,   95
And bury me in flames ! sweats hot as sulphur
Boil through my pores ! affliction hath in store
No torture like to this.

*Org.*               Behold a patience !
Lay-by thy whining gray dissimulation,
Do something worth a chronicle ; show justice   100
Upon the author of this mischief ; dig out
The jealousies that hatched this thraldom first
With thine own poniard : every antic rapture
Can roar as thine does.

*Ith.*               Orgilus, forbear.

*Bass.*   Disturb him not ; it is a talking motion
Provided for my torment.   What a fool am I   106
To bandy passion ! ere I'll speak a word,
I will look on and burst.

*Pen.*               I loved you once.   [*To* ORGILUS.

*Org.* Thou didst, wronged creature : in despite of
    malice,
For it I love thee ever.

*Pen.* Spare your hand ; 110
Believe me, I'll not hurt it,

*Org.* My heart too.

*Pen.* Complain not though I wring it hard : I'll
    kiss it ;
O, 'tis a fine soft palm !—hark, in thine ear ;
Like whom do I look, prithee ?—nay, no whispering.
Goodness ! we had been happy ; too much happiness
Will make folk proud, they say—but that is he— 116
                    [*Pointing to* ITHOCLES.
And yet he paid for't home ; alas, his heart
Is crept into the cabinet of the princess ;
We shall have points and bride-laces. Remember,
When we last gathered roses in the garden, 120
I found my wits ; but truly you lost yours.
That's he, and still 'tis he.
                [*Again pointing to* ITHOCLES.

*Ith.* Poor soul, how idly
Her fancies guide her tongue !

*Bass.* [*aside*] Keep in, vexation,
And break not into the clamour.

*Org.* [*aside*] She has tutored me,
Some powerful inspiration checks my laziness.— 125
Now let me kiss your hand, grieved beauty.

*Pen.* Kiss it.—
Alack, alack, his lips be wondrous cold ;
Dear soul, has lost his colour : have ye seen

A straying heart ? all crannies ! every drop
Of blood is turnèd to an amethyst,                    130
Which married bachelors hang in their ears.

 *Org.*  Peace usher her into Elysium !—
If this be madness, madness is an oracle.
[Aside, and exit.

 *Ith.*  Christalla, Philema, when slept my sister,
Her ravings are so wild ?
 *Chris.*       Sir, not these ten days. 135
 *Phil.*  We watch by her continually ; besides,
We can not any way pray her to eat.
 *Bass.*  O, misery of miseries !
 *Pen.*        Take comfort ;
You may live well, and die a good old man :
By yea and nay, an oath not to be broken,              140
If you had joined our hands once in the temple,—
'Twas since my father died, for had he lived
He would have done't,—I must have called you
   father,—
O, my wrecked honour ! ruined by those tyrants,
A cruel brother and a desperate dotage               145
There is no peace left for a ravished wife
Widowed by lawless marriage ; to all memory
Penthea's, poor Penthea's name is strumpeted :
But since her blood was seasoned by the forfeit
Of noble shame with mixtures of pollution,           150
Her blood—'tis just—be henceforth never heightened
With taste of sustenance ! starve ; let that fulness
Whose plurisy hath fevered faith and modesty—
Forgive me ; O, I faint !
[Falls into the arms of her Attendants.

*Arm.* Be not so wilful,
Sweet niece, to work thine own destruction.

*Ith.* Nature
Will call her daughter monster !—What ! not eat ?
Refuse the only ordinary means
Which are ordained for life ?  Be not, my sister,
A murderess to thyself.—Hear'st thou this, Bassanes ?

*Bass.*  Foh ! I am busy ;. for I have not thoughts
Enow to think : all shall be well anon.          161
'Tis tumbling in my head ; there is a mastery
In art to fatten and keep smooth the outside,
Yes, and to comfort-up the vital spirits
Without the help of food, fumes or perfumes,     165
Perfumes or fumes.  Let her alone ; I'll search out
The trick on't

*Pen.*          Lead me gently ; heavens reward ye.
Griefs are sure friends ; they leave without control
Nor cure nor comforts for a leprous soul.
          [*Exit, supported by* CHRISTALLA *and* PHILEMA.

*Bass.*  I grant ye ; and will put in practice instantly
What you shall still admire : 'tis wonderful,     171
'Tis super-singular, not to be matched ;
Yet, when I've done't, I've done't :—ye shall all
     thank me.                    [*Exit.*

*Arm.*  The sight is full of terror.

*Ith.*                    On my soul
Lies such an infinite clog of massy dulness,      175
As that I have not sense enough to feel it.—
See, uncle, the angry thing returns again ;
Shall's welcome him with thunder ? we are haunted,

And must use exorcism to conjure down
This spirit of malevolence.

*Arm.*                         Mildly, nephew.      180

*Enter* NEARCHUS *and* AMELUS.

*Near.*  I come not, sir, to chide your late disorder,
Admitting that the inurement to a roughness
In soldiers of your years and fortunes, chiefly
So lately prosperous, hath not yet shook off
The custom of the war in hours of leisure ;       185
Nor shall you need excuse, since you're to render
Account to that fair excellence, the princess,
Who in her private gallery expects it
From your own mouth alone : I am a messenger
But to her pleasure.

*Ith.*                    Excellent Nearchus,      190
Be prince still of my services, and conquer
Without the combat of dispute ; I honour ye.

*Near.*  The king is on a sudden indisposed,
Physicians are called for ; 'twere fit, Armostes,
You should be near him.

*Arm.*                    Sir, I kiss your hands.   195
                    [*Exeunt* ITHOCLES *and* ARMOSTES.

*Near.*  Amelus, I perceive Calantha's bosom
Is warmed with other fires than such as can
Take strength from any fuel of the love
I might address to her : young Ithocles,
Or ever I mistake, is lord ascendant              200
Of her devotions ; one, to speak him truly,
In every disposition nobly fashioned.

*Ame.*   But can your highness brook to be so rivalled,
Considering the inequality of the persons?

*Near.*   I can, Amelus; for affections injured   205
By tyranny or rigour of compulsion,
Like tempest-threatened trees unfirmly rooted,
Ne'er spring to timely growth: observe, for instance,
Life-spent Penthea and unhappy Orgilus.

*Ame.*   How does your grace determine?

*Near.*                            To be jealous
In public of what privately I'll further;        211
And though they shall not know, yet they shall find it.
                                        [*Exeunt.*

SCENE III.   *An Apartment in the Palace.*

*Enter* AMYCLAS, *led by* HEMOPHIL *and* GRONEAS, *followed by* ARMOSTES *with a box,* CROTOLON, *and* PROPHILUS. AMYCLAS *is placed in a chair.*

*Amy.*   Our daughter is not near?

*Arm.*                             She is retired, sir,
Into her gallery.

*Amy.*          Where's the prince our cousin?

*Pro.*   New walked into the grove, my lord.

*Amy.*                              All leave us
Except Armostes, and you, Crotolon;
We would be private.

*Pro.*                 Health unto your majesty!   5
        [*Exeunt* PROPHILUS, HEMOPHIL, *and* GRONEAS.

*Amy.*   What! Tecnicus is gone?

*Arm.*                                    He is to Delphos ;
And to your royal hands presents this box.

*Amy.*    Unseal it, good Armostes ; therein lie
The secrets of the oracle ; out with it :
                              [ASMOSTES *takes out the scroll.*
Apollo live our patron !  Read, Armostes.          10

*Arm.* [*reads*]
      " The plot in which the vine takes root
        Begins to dry from head to foot ;
        The stock, soon withering, want of sap
        Doth cause to quail the budding grape ;
        But from the neighbouring elm a dew          15
        Shall drop, and feed the plot anew."

*Amy.*    That is the oracle : what exposition
Makes the philosopher ?

*Arm.*                      This brief one only. [*Reads.*
" The plot is Sparta, the dried vine the king ;
  The quailing grape his daughter ; but the thing   20
  Of most importance, not to be revealed,
  Is a near prince, the elm : the rest concealed.
                              TECNICUS."

*Amy.*    Enough ; although the opening of this riddle
Be but itself a riddle, yet we construe
How near our labouring age draws to a rest :        25
But must Calantha quail too ? that young grape
Untimely budded !  I could mourn for her ;
Her tenderness hath yet deserved no rigour
So to be crossed by fate.

*Arm.*                    You misapply, sir,—
With favour let me speak it,—what Apollo            30
Hath clouded in hid sense : I here conjecture

Her marriage with some neighbouring prince, the
    dew
Of which befriending elm shall ever strengthen
Your subjects with a sovereignity of power.

    *Crot.* Besides, most gracious lord, the pith of
      oracles                              35
Is to be then digested when the events
Expound their truth, not brought as soon to light
As uttered ; Truth is child of Time : and herein
I find no scruple, rather cause of comfort,
With unity of kingdoms.

    *Amy.*                  May it prove so,    40
For weal of this dear nation !—Where is Ithocles ?—
Armostes, Crotolon, when this withered vine
Of my frail carcass, on the funeral pile
Is fired into its ashes, let that young man
Be hedged about still with your cares and loves :  45
Much owe I to his worth, much to his service,—
Let such as wait come in now.

    *Arm.*                  All attend here !

*Enter* CALANTHA, ITHOCLES, PROPHILUS, ORGILUS,
    EUPHRANEA, HEMOPHIL, *and* GRONEAS.

    *Cal.* Dear sir ! king ! father !

    *Ith.*                 O, my royal master !

    *Amy.* Cleave not my heart, sweet twins of my life's
      solace,
With your forejudging fears ; there is no physic  50
So cunningly restorative to cherish
The fall of age, or call back youth and vigour,
As your consents in duty : I will shake off

This languishing disease of time, to quicken
Fresh pleasures in these drooping hours of sadness.
Is fair Euphranea married yet to Prophilus ?  56

 *Crot.*  This morning, gracious lord.

 *Org.*        This very morning ;
Which, with your highness' leave, you may observe
 too.
Our sister looks, methinks, mirthful and sprightly,
As if her chaster fancy could already  60
Expound the riddle of her gain in losing
A trifle maids know only that they know not.
Pish ! prithee, blush not ; 'tis but honest change
Of fashion in the garment, loose for strait,
And so the modest maid is made a wife :  65
Shrewd business—is't not, sister ?

 *Euph.*       You are pleasant.

 *Amy.*  We thank thee, Orgilus ; this mirth becomes
 thee.
But wherefore sits the court in such a silence ?
A wedding without revels is not seemly.

 *Cal.*  Your late indisposition, sir, forbade it.  70

 *Amy.*  Be it thy charge, Calantha, to set forward
The bridal sports, to which I will be present ;
If not, at least consenting.—Mine own Ithocles,
I have done little for thee yet.

 *Ith.*       You've built me
To the full height I stand in.

 *Cal.* [*aside*]    Now or never !—  75
May I propose a suit ?

 *Amy.*     Demand, and have it.

*Cal.* Pray, sir, give me this young man, and no
    further
Account him yours than he deserves in all things
To be thought worthy mine : I will esteem him
According to his merit.

*Amy.*               Still thou'rt my daughter,
Still grow'st upon my heart.—[*To* ITHOCLES] Give
    me thine hand ;—                     81
Calantha, take thine own : in noble actions
Thou'lt find him firm and absolute.—I would not
Have parted with thee, Ithocles, to any
But to a mistress who is all what I am.       85

  *Ith.* A change, great king, most wished for, 'cause
    the same.

  *Cal.* [*aside to* ITHOCLES] Thou'rt mine. Have I
    now kept my word ?

  *Ith.* [*aside to* CALANTHA]            Divinely.

  *Org.* Rich fortunes guard, the favour of the
    princess
Rock thee, brave man, in ever-crownèd plenty !
You're minion of the time ; be thankful for it.—   90
[*Aside*] Ho ! here's a swing in destiny—apparent !
The youth is up on tiptoe, yet may stumble.

  *Amy.* On to your recreations.—Now convey me
Unto my bed-chamber : none on his forehead
Wear a distempered look.

  *All.*              The gods preserve ye !   95

  *Cal.* [*aside to* ITHOCLES] Sweet, be not from my
    sight.

*Ith.* [*aside to* CALANTHA]  My whole felicity!
[AMYCLAS *is carried out.  Exeunt all but*
ITHOCLES, *who is detained by* ORGILUS.

*Org.*  Shall I be bold, my lord ?

*Ith.*  Thou canst not, Orgilus.
Call me thine own ; for Prophilus must henceforth
Be all thy sister's : friendship, though it cease not
In marriage, yet is oft at less command  100
Than when a single freedom can dispose it.

*Org.*  Most right, my most good lord, my most
  great lord,
My gracious princely lord, I might add, royal.

*Ith.*  Royal ! a subject royal ?

*Org.*  Why not, pray, sir ?
The sovereignity of kingdoms in their nonage  105
Stooped to desert, not birth ; there's as much merit
In clearness of affection as in puddle
Of generation ; you have conquered love
Even in the loveliest ; if I greatly err not,
The son of Venus hath bequeathed his quiver  110
To Ithocles his manage, by whose arrows
Calantha's breast is opened.

*Ith.*  Can't be possible ?

*Org.*  I was myself a piece of suitor once,
And forward in preferment too ; so forward,
That, speaking truth, I may without offence, sir,  115
Presume to whisper that my hopes, and—hark ye—
My certainty of marriage stood assured
With as firm footing—by your leave—as any's
Now at this very instant—but—

*Ith.*                                    'Tis granted :
And for a league of privacy between us,              120
Read o'er my bosom and partake a secret ;
The princess is contracted mine.

*Org.*                          Still, why not ?
I now applaud her wisdom : when your kingdom
Stands seated in your will secure and settled,
I dare pronounce you will be a just monarch ;      125
Greece must admire and tremble.

*Ith.*                              Then the sweetness
Of so imparadised a comfort, Orgilus !
It is to banquet with the gods.

*Org.*                          The glory
Of numerous children, potency of nobles,
Bent knees, hearts paved to tread on !

*Ith.*                          With a friendship
So dear, so fast as thine.

*Org.*                      I am unfitting              131
For office ; but for service—

*Ith.*                          We'll distinguish
Our fortunes merely in the title ; partners
In all respects else but the bed.

*Org.*                          The bed !
Forfend it Jove's own jealousy !—till lastly      135
We slip down in the common earth together ;
And there our beds are equal ; save some monu-
    ment
To show this was the king, and this the subject.—

                          [*Soft, sad music.*
List, what sad sounds are these,—extremely sad ones ?

*Ith.*   Sure, from Penthea's lodgings.

*Org.*                                   Hark ! a voice too.

SONG *within.*

O, no more, no more, too late                    141
   Sighs are spent ; the burning tapers
Of a life as chaste as fate,
   Pure as are unwritten papers,
Are burnt out : no heat, no light              145
Now remains ; 'tis ever night.

Love is dead ; let lover's eyes,
   Locked in endless dreams,
   Th' extremes of all extremes,
Ope no more, for now Love dies,              150
Now Love dies,—implying
Love's martyrs must be ever, ever dying.

*Ith.*   O, my misgiving heart !

*Org.*                                   A horrid stillness
Succeeds this deathful air ; let's know the reason :
Tread softly ; there is mystery in mourning. [*Exeunt.*

SCENE IV.   PENTHEA'S *Apartment in the Palace.*

PENTHEA *discovered in a chair, veiled ;* CHRISTALLA
   *and* PHILEMA *at her feet mourning. Enter two*
   Servants *with two other chairs, one with an engine.*

*Enter* ITHOCLES *and* ORGILUS.

*1st Ser.* [*aside to* ORGILUS] 'Tis done ; that on her
   right hand.

*Org.*            Good : begone.   [*Exeunt Servants.*

*Ith.*   Soft peace enrich this room !

*Org.*                         How fares this lady ?

*Phil.*   Dead !

*Chris.*         Dead !

*Phil.*               Starved !

*Chris.*                   Starved !

*Ith.*                           Me miserable !

*Org.*                               Tell us
How parted she from life.

*Phil.*                     She called for music,
And begged some gentle voice to tune a farewell     5
To life and griefs : Christalla touched the lute ;
I wept the funeral song.

*Chris.*                   Which scarce was ended
But her last breath sealed-up these hollow sounds,
" O, cruel Ithocles and injured Orgilus ! "
So down she drew her veil, so died.

*Ith.*                         So died !     10

*Org.*   Up ! you are messengers of death ; go
     from us ;          [CHRISTALLA *and* PHILEMA *rise.*
Here's woe enough to court without a prompter :
Away ; and—hark ye—till you see us next,
No syllable that she is dead.—Away,
Keep a smooth brow.

                    [*Exeunt* CHRISTALLA *and* PHILEMA.
                    My lord,—

*Ith.*                     Mine only sister !     15
Another is not left me.

*Org.*               Take that chair ;
I'll seat me here in this : between us sits

The object of our sorrows ; some few tears
We'll part among us ; I perhaps can mix
One lamentable story to prepare 'em.—      20
There, there ; sit there, my lord.

   *Ith.*                  Yes, as you please.

            [*Sits down, the chair closes upon him.*
What means this treachery ?

   *Org.*             Caught ! you are caught,
Young master ; 'tis thy throne of coronation,
Thou fool of greatness !  See, I take this veil off ;
Survey a beauty withered by the flames      25
Of an insulting Phaëton, her brother.

   *Ith.*   Thou mean'st to kill me basely ?

   *Org.*               I foreknew
The last act of her life, and trained thee hither
To sacrifice a tyrant to a turtle.
You dreamt of kingdoms, did ye ? how to bosom  30
The delicacies of a youngling princess ;
How with this nod to grace that subtle courtier,
How with that frown to make this noble tremble,
And so forth ; while Penthea's groans and tortures,
Her agonies, her miseries, afflictions,     35
Ne'er touched upon your thought : as for my injuries,
Alas, they were beneath your royal pity ;
But yet they lived, thou proud man, to confound thee.
Behold thy fate ; this steel !      [*Draws a dagger.*

   *Ith.*           Strike home !  A courage
As keen as thy revenge shall give it welcome :   40
But prithee faint not ; if the wound close up,
Tent it with double force, and search it deeply.
Thou look'st that I should whine and beg compassion,

As loth to leave the vainness of my glories ;
A statelier resolution arms my confidence,               45
To cozen thee of honour ; neither could I
With equal trial of unequal fortune
By hazard of a duel ; 'twere a bravery
Too mighty for a slave intending murder.
On to the execution, and inherit                         50
A conflict with thy horrors.

   *Org.*             By Apollo,
Thou talk'st a goodly language ! for requital
I will report thee to thy mistress richly :
And take this peace along ; some few short minutes
Determined, my resolves shall quickly follow           55
Thy wrathful ghost ; then, if we tug for mastery,
Penthea's sacred eyes shall lend new courage.
Give me thy hand : be healthful in thy parting
From lost mortality ! thus, thus I free it.   [*Stabs him.*

   *Ith.*   Yet, yet, I scorn to shrink.

   *Org.*            Keep up thy spirit :
I will be gentle even in blood ; to linger              61
Pain, which I strive to cure, were to be cruel.

                      [*Stabs him again.*

   *Ith.*   Nimble in vengeance, I forgive thee.   Follow
Safety, with best success : O, may it prosper !—
Penthea, by thy side thy brother bleeds ;               65
The earnest of his wrongs to thy forced faith.
Thoughts of ambition, or delicious banquet
With beauty, youth, and love, together perish
In my last breath, which on the sacred altar
Of a long-looked-for peace—now—moves—to heaven.
                      [*Dies.*

*Org.*   Farewell, fair spring of manhood ! henceforth
    welcome                                        71
Best expectation of a noble sufferance.
I'll lock the bodies safe, till what must follow
Shall be approved.—Sweet twins, shine stars for-
    ever !—
In vain they build their hopes whose life is shame :
No monument lasts but a happy name.              76
                [*Locks the door, and exit.*

# ACT THE FIFTH.

### Scene I. *A Room in* Bassanes' *House.*

#### *Enter* Bassanes.

*Bass.*   Athens—to Athens I have sent, the nursery
Of Greece for learning and the fount of knowledge ;
For here in Sparta there's not left amongst us
One wise man to direct ; we're all turned madcaps.
'Tis said Apollo is the god of herbs,                         5
Then certainly he knows the virtue of 'em :
To Delphos I have sent too.   If there can be
A help for nature, we are sure yet.

#### *Enter* Orgilus.

*Org.*                                    Honour
Attend thy counsels ever !

*Bass.*                          I beseech thee
With all my heart, let me go from thee quietly ;      10
I will not aught to do with thee, of all men.
The doubles of a hair,—or, in a morning,
Salutes from a splay-footed witch,—to drop
Three drops of blood at th' nose just and no more,—
Croaking of ravens, or the screech of owls,            15
Are not so boding mischief as thy crossing
My private meditations : shun me, prithee ;
And if I cannot love thee heartily,
I'll love thee as well as I can.

*Org.*                              Noble Bassanes,
Mistake me not.

    *Bass.*          Phew ! then we shall be troubled.    20
Thou wert ordained my plague—heaven make me
    thankful,
And give me patience too, heaven, I beseech thee.

    *Org.*  Accept a league of amity ; for henceforth,
I vow, by my best genius, in a syllable,
Never to speak vexation ; I will study          25
Service and friendship, with a zealous sorrow
For my past incivility towards ye.

    *Bass.*  Hey-day, good words, good words ! I must
    believe 'em,
And be a coxcomb for my labour.

    *Org.*                              Use not
So hard a language ; your misdoubt is causeless :    30
For instance, if you promise to put on
A constancy of patience, such a patience
As chronicle or history ne'er mentioned,
As follows not example, but shall stand
A wonder and a theme for imitation,             35
The first, the index pointing to a second,
I will acquaint ye with an unmatched secret,
Whose knowledge to your griefs shall set a period.

    *Bass.*  Thou canst not, Orgilus ; 'tis in the power
Of the gods only : yet, for satisfaction,           40
Because I note an earnest in thine utterance,
Unforced and naturally free, be resolute.
The virgin-bays shall not withstand the lightning
With a more careless danger than my constancy
The full of thy relation ; could it move           45

Distraction in a senseless marble statue,
It should find me a rock : I do expect now
Some truth of unheard moment.

*Org.*　　　　　　　　　To your patience
You must add privacy, as strong in silence
As mysteries locked-up in Jove's own bosom.　　50

*Bass.*　A skull hid in the earth a treble age
Shall sooner prate.

*Org.*　　　　　　Lastly, to such direction
As the severity of a glorious action
Deserves to lead your wisdom and your judgment,
You ought to yield obedience.

*Bass.*　　　　　　　　With assurance　55
Of will and thankfulness.

*Org.*　　　　　　　With manly courage
Please, then, to follow me.

*Bass.*　·　　　　　Where'er, I fear not. [*Exeunt.*


SCENE II.　*A State-room in the Palace.*


*A flourish.　Enter* EUPHRANEA *led by* GRONEAS *and*
HEMOPHIL ; PROPHILUS, *led by* CHRISTALLA *and*
PHILEMA ; NEARCHUS *supporting* CALANTHA ;
CROTOLON *and* AMELUS.


*Cal.*　We miss our servant Ithocles and Orgilus ;
On whom attend they ?

*Crot.*　　　　　　My son, gracious princess,
Whispered some new device, to which these revels
Should be but usher : wherein I conceive
Lord Ithocles and he himself are actors.　　5

*Cal.* A fair excuse for absence : as for Bassanes,
Delights to him are troublesome : Armostes
Is with the king ?

*Crot.* He is.

*Cal.* On to the dance !—
Dear cousin, hand you the bride ; the bridegroom must be
Intrusted to my courtship. Be not jealous,     10
Euphranea ; I shall scarcely prove a temptress.—
Fall to our dance.

*The Revels.*

*Music.* NEARCHUS *dances with* EUPHRANEA, PRO-
PHILUS *with* CALANTHA, CHRISTALLA *with* HEMO-
PHIL, PHILEMA *with* GRONEAS.

*They dance the first change ; during which* ARMOSTES
*enters.*

*Arm.* [*whispers* CALANTHA] The king your
father's dead.

*Cal.* To the other change.

*Arm.* Is't possible ?

*They dance the second change.*

*Enter* BASSANES.

*Bass.* [*whispers* CALANTHA] O, madam !
Penthea, poor Penthea's starved.

*Cal.* Beshrew thee !—
Lead to the next.

*Bass.* Amazement dulls my senses.     15

*They dance the third change.*

*Enter* ORGILUS.

*Org.* [*whispers* CALANTHA] Brave Ithocles is
murdered, murdered cruelly.

*Cal.* How dull this music sounds! Strike up
  more sprightly ;
Our footings are not active like our heart,
Which treads the nimbler measure.

*Org.*                                1 am thunderstruck.

*The last change.*

*Cal.* So! let us breathe awhile.  [*Music ceases.*]—
  Hath not this motion                              21
Raised fresher colour on our cheeks ?

*Near.*                                Sweet princess,
A perfect purity of blood enamels
The beauty of your white.

*Cal.*                                We all look cheerfully :
And, cousin, 'tis methinks a rare presumption
In any who prefer our lawful pleasures              25
Before their own sour censure, t' interrupt
The custom of this ceremony bluntly.

*Near.*  None dares, lady.

*Cal.*  Yes, yes ; some hollow voice delivered to me
How that the king was dead.

*Arm.*                                The king is dead :  30
That fatal news was mine ; for in mine arms
He breathed his last, and with his crown bequeathed
  ye
Your mother's wedding-ring ; which here I tender.

*Crot.*  Most strange !

*Cal.*  Peace crown his ashes !  We are queen, then.

*Near.*  Long live Calantha !  Sparta's sovereign
    queen !                                                        35

*All.*  Long live the queen !

*Cal.*                             What whispered Bassanes ?

*Bass.*  That my Penthea, miserable soul,
Was starved to death.

*Cal.*                          She's happy ; she hath finished
A long and painful progress.—A third murmur
Pierced mine unwilling ears.

*Org.*                               That Ithocles          40
Was murdered ;—rather butchered, had not bravery
Of an undaunted spirit, conquering terror,
Proclaimed his last act triumph over ruin.

*Arm.*  How ! murdered !

*Cal.*              By whose hand ?

*Org.*                              By mine ; this weapon
Was instrument to my revenge : the reasons          45
Are just, and known ; quit him of these, and then
Never lived gentleman of greater merit,
Hope or abiliment to steer a kingdom.

*Crot.*  Fie, Orgilus !

*Euph.*              Fie, brother !

*Cal.*                          You have done it ?

*Bass.*  How it was done let him report, the forfeit
Of whose allegiance to our laws doth covet          51
Rigour of justice ; but that done it is
Mine eyes have been an evidence of credit
Too sure to be convinced.  Armostes, rend not

Thine arteries with hearing the bare circumstances
Of these calamities ; thou'st lost a nephew, 　　56
A niece, and I a wife : continue man still ;
Make me the pattern of digesting evils,
Who can outlive my mighty ones, not shrinking
At such a pressure as would sink a soul 　　60
Into what's most of death, the worst of horrors.
But I have sealed a covenant with sadness,
And entered into bonds without condition,
To stand these tempests calmly ; mark me, nobles,
I do not shed a tear, not for Penthea ! 　　65
Excellent misery !

*Cal.* 　　　　　We begin our reign
With a first act of justice : thy confession,
Unhappy Orgilus, dooms thee a sentence ;
But yet thy father's or thy sister's presence
Shall be excused.—Give, Crotolon, a blessing 　　70
To thy lost son ;—Euphranea, take a farewell ;—
And both be gone.

*Crot.* [*to* Orgilus.] Confirm thee noble sorrow
In worthy resolution !

*Euph.* 　　　　　Could my tears speak,
My griefs were slight.

*Org.* 　　　　　All goodness dwell amongst ye !
Enjoy my sister, Prophilus : my vengeance 　　75
Aimed never at thy prejudice.

*Cal.* 　　　　　　　Now withdraw.
[*Exeunt* Crotolon, Prophilus, *and* Euphranea.
Bloody relater of thy stains in blood,
For that thou hast reported him, whose fortunes
And life by thee are both at once snatched from him,

With honourable mention, make thy choice     80
Of what death likes thee best; there's all our
    bounty.—
But to excuse delays, let me, dear cousin,
Intreat you and these lords see execution
Instant before ye part.

    *Near.*         Your will commands us.

    *Org.* One suit, just queen, my last; vouchsafe
    your clemency,         85
That by no common hand I be divided
From this my humble frailty.

    *Cal.*         To their wisdoms
Who are to be spectators of thine end
I make the reference : those that are dead
Are dead ; had they not now died, of necessity     90
They must have paid the debt they owed to nature
One time or other.—Use dispatch, my lords ;
We'll suddenly prepare our coronation.

    [*Exeunt* CALANTHA, PHILEMA, *and* CHRISTALLA.

    *Arm.* 'Tis strange these tragedies should never
    touch on
Her female pity.

    *Bass.*         She has a masculine spirit;     95
And wherefore should I pule, and, like a girl,
Put finger in the eye ? let's be all toughness,
Without distinction betwixt sex and sex.

    *Near.* Now, Orgilus, thy choice ?

    *Org.*         To bleed to death.

    *Arm.* The executioner ?

    *Org.*         Myself, no surgeon ;     100

I am well skilled in letting blood.   Bind fast
This arm, that so the pipes may from their conduits
Convey a full stream ;  here's a skilful instrument ;
                      [*Shows his dagger.*
Only I am a beggar to some charity
To speed me in this execution                                     105
By lending th' other prick to the tother arm,
When this is bubbling life out.

   *Bass.*                 I am for ye ;
It most concerns my art, my care, my credit.—
Quick fillet both his arms.

   *Org.*             Grammercy, friendship !
Such courtesies are real which flow cheerfully        110
Without an expectation of requital.
Reach me a staff in this hand.   [*They give him a staff.*]
    —If a proneness
Or custom in my nature from my cradle
Had been inclined to fierce and eager bloodshed,
A coward guilt, hid in a coward quaking,               115
Would have betrayed me to ignoble flight
And vagabond pursuit of dreadful safety :
But look upon my steadiness, and scorn not
The sickness of my fortune, which since Bassanes
Was husband to Penthea had lain bed-rid.               120
We trifle time in words :—thus I show cunning
In opening of a vein too full, too lively.
               [*Pierces the vein with his dagger.*
   *Arm.*   Desperate courage !
   *Near.*             Honourable infamy !
   *Hem.*   I tremble at the sight.
   *Gro.*             Would I were loose !

*Bass.* It sparkles like a lusty wine new broached ;
The vessel must be sound from which it issues.—
Grasp hard this other stick—I'll be as nimble—
But prithee, look not pale—have at ye ! stretch out
Thine arm with vigour and with unshook virtue.

[Opens the vein.

Good ! O, I envy not a rival, fitted       130
To conquer in extremities : this pastime
Appears majestical ; some high-tuned poem
Hereafter shall deliver to posterity
The writer's glory and his subject's triumph.
How is't, man ?—droop not yet.

*Org.*             I feel no palsies.
On a pair-royal do I wait in death ;       136
My sovereign, as his liegeman ; on my mistress,
As a devoted servant ; and on Ithocles,
As if no brave, yet no unworthy enemy :
Nor did I use an engine to entrap       140
His life, out of a slavish fear to combat
Youth, strength, or cunning ; but for that I durst not
Engage the goodness of a cause on fortune,
By which his name might have outfaced my venge-
    ance.
O, Tecnicus, inspired with Phœbus' fire !       145
I call to mind thy augury, 'twas perfect ;
" Revenge proves its own executioner."
When feeble man is bending to his mother,
The dust he was first framed on, thus he totters.

*Bass.* Life's fountain is dried up.

*Org.*             So falls the standard
Of my prerogative in being a creature !       151

A mist hangs o'er mine eyes, the sun's bright splen-
  dour
Is clouded in an everlasting shadow ;
Welcome, thou ice, that sitt'st about my heart,
No heat can ever thaw thee.                    [*Dies.*

  *Near.*                    Speech hath left him.   155
  *Bass.*   He has shook hands with time ; his funeral
  `urn
Shall be my charge : remove the bloodless body.
The coronation must require attendance ;
That past, my few days can be but one mourning.
                                      [*Exeunt.*


### SCENE III.   *A Temple.*

*An altar covered with white ; two lights of virgin wax
  upon it.   Recorders play, during which enter Attendants bearing* ITHOCLES *on a hearse (in a rich
  robe, with a crown on his head) and place him on one
  side of the altar.   Afterwards enter* CALANTHA *in
  white, crowned, attended by* EUPHRANEA, PHILEMA,
  *and* CHRISTALLA, *also in white ;* NEARCHUS,
  ARMOSTES.   CROTOLON, PROPHILUS, AMELUS,
  BASSANES, HEMOPHIL, *and* GRONEAS.*

CALANTHA *kneels before the altar, the* Ladies *kneeling
  behind her, the rest stand off.   The recorders cease
  during her devotions.   Soft music.* CALANTHA
  *and the rest rise, doing obeisance to the altar.*

  *Cal.*   Our orisons are heard ; the gods are merci-
  ful.—
Now tell me, you whose loyalties pay tribute
To us your lawful sovereign, how unskilful

Your duties or obedience is to render
Subjection to the sceptre of a virgin,                          5
Who have been ever fortunate in princes
Of masculine and stirring composition.
A woman has enough to govern wisely
Her own demeanours, passions, and divisions.
A nation warlike and inured to practice          10
Of policy and labour cannot brook
A feminate authority : we therefore
Command your counsel, how you may advise us
In choosing of a husband, whose abilities
Can better guide this kingdom.

   *Near.*                        Royal lady,          15
Your law is in your will.

   *Arm.*                     We have seen tokens
Of constancy too lately to mistrust it.

   *Crot.*   Yet, if your highness settle on a choice
By your own judgment both allowed and liked of,
Sparta may grow in power, and proceed          20
To an increasing height.

   *Cal.*                  Hold you the same mind ?

   *Bass.*   Alas, great mistress, reason is so clouded
With the thick darkness of my infinite woes,
That I forecast nor dangers, hopes, or safety.
Give me some corner of the world to wear out          25
The remnant of the minutes I must number,
Where I may hear no sounds but sad complaints
Of virgins who have lost contracted partners ;
Of husbands howling that their wives were ravished
By some untimely fate ; of friends divided          30
By churlish opposition ; or of fathers

Weeping upon their children's slaughter'd carcasses ;
Or daughters groaning o'er their fathers' hearses ;
And I can dwell there, and with these keep consort
As musical as theirs.  What can you look for        35
From an old, foolish, peevish, doting man
But craziness of age ?

  *Cal.*  Cousin of Argos,—

  *Near.*                 Madam ?

  *Cal.*                      Were I presently
To choose you for my lord, I'll open freely
What articles I would propose to treat on
Before our marriage.

  *Near.*           Name them, virtuous lady.  40

  *Cal.*  I would presume you would retain the royalty
Of Sparta in her own bounds ; then in Argos
Armostes might be viceroy ; in Messene
Might Crotolon bear sway ; and Bassanes—

  *Bass.*  I, queen ! alas, what I ?

  *Cal.*             Be Sparta's marshal :  45
The multitudes of high employments could not
But set a peace to private griefs.  These gentlemen,
Groneas and Hemophil, with worthy pensions,
Should wait upon your person in your chamber.—
I would bestow Christalla on Amelus.            50
She'll prove a constant wife ; and Philema
Should into Vesta's Temple.

  *Bass.*         This is a testament !
It sounds not like conditions on a marriage.

  *Near.*  All this should be performed.

  *Cal.*           Lastly, for Prophilus,

He should be, cousin, solemnly invested 55
In all those honours, titles, and preferments
Which his dear friend and my neglected husband
Too short a time enjoyed.

    *Cro.*            I am unworthy
To live in your remembrance.

    *Euph.*               Excellent lady!

    *Near.*   Madam, what means that word, " neglected
    husband " ?                         60

    *Cal.*  Forgive me :—now I turn to thee, thou
    shadow
Of my contracted lord !  Bear witness all,
I put my mother's wedding-ring upon
His finger ; 'twas my father's last bequest.
             [*Places a ring on the finger of* ITHOCLES.
Thus I new-marry him whose wife I am ; 65
Death shall not separate us.  O, my lords,
I but deceived your eyes with antic gesture,
When one news straight came huddling on another
Of death ! and death ! and death ! still I danced for-
    ward ;
But it struck home, and here, and in an instant.  70
Be such mere women, who with shrieks and outcries
Can vow a present end to all their sorrows,
Yet live to court new pleasures and outlive them :
They are the silent griefs which cut the heart-strings;
Let me die smiling.

    *Near.*           'Tis a truth too ominous.  75

    *Cal.*  One kiss on these cold lips, my last ! [*Kisses*
    ITHOCLES.]—Crack, crack !—
Argos now's Sparta's king.—Command the voices

Which wait at the altar now to sing the song
I fitted for my end.

   *Near.*            Sirs, the song !

### DIRGE.

   *Chor.*   Glories, pleasures, pomps, delights, and
       ease,

                Can but please        81
           The outward senses, when the mind
           Is or untroubled or by peace refined.

*1st. Voice.* Crowns may flourish and decay
           Beauties shine, but fade away.     85

*2nd Voice.* Youth may revel, yes it must
           Lie down in a bed of dust.

*3rd Voice.* Earthly honours flow and waste,
           Time alone doth change and last.

   *Chor.* Sorrows mingled with contents prepare
                Rest for care ;        91
           Love only reigns in death ; though art
           Can find no comfort for a broken heart.

                   [CALANTHA *dies.*

   *Arm.*   Look to the queen !

   *Bass.*             Her heart is broke indeed.
O, royal maid, would thou hadst missed this part !
Yet 'twas a brave one.   I must weep to see    96
Her smile in death.

   *Arm.*            Wise Tecnicus ! thus said he ;
" When youth is ripe, and age from time doth part,
The Lifeless Trunk shall wed the Broken Heart."
'Tis here fulfilled.

*Near.*　　　　　I am your king.

*All.*　　　　　　　　　Long live 100
Nearchus, King of Sparta !

*Near.*　　　　　　Her last will
Shall never be digressed from : wait in order
Upon these faithful lovers, as become us.—
The counsels of the gods are never known
Till men call the effects of them their own.　[*Exeunt.*


## EPILOGUE.

WHERE noble judgments and clear eyes are fixed
To grace endeavour, there sits truth, not mixed
With ignorance ; those censures may command
Belief which talk not till they understand.
Let some say, " This was flat ; " some, " Here the scene 5
Fell from its height ; " another, " That the mean
Was ill observed in such a growing passion
As it transcended either state or fashion : "
Some few may cry, " 'Twas pretty well," or so,
" But—" and there shrug in silence : yet we know
Our writer's aim was in the whole addrest 11
Well to deserve of all, but please the best ;
Which granted, by the allowance of this strain
The BROKEN HEART may be pieced-up again.

# NOTES.

# NOTES.

*The text of this edition is, in the main, that of Gifford, as amended by Dyce.*

*The heavy figures refer to the pages of the text; the lighter figures to the lines.*

Of the first appearance or of the success of the play, there is no extant account. The title-page of the original quarto is given in substance below :

## THE BROKEN HEART.

### A Tragedy.

### ACTED

By the KING'S Majesties Seruants
at the priuate Houfe in the
### BLACK-FRIERS.

*Fide Honor.*

### LONDON:

Printed by I. B. for HVGH BEESTON,
and are to be fold at his shop, neere
the Caftle in Corne-hill. *1633.*

The motto, *Fide Honor*, appears on several other of Ford's title-pages. It is an anagram of his own name as he sometimes spelled it, *Iohn Forde.*

The tragedy was dedicated to "the most worthy deserver of the noblest titles in honour, William, Lord Craven, Baron of Hampsted-Marshall." This nobleman who, according to Gifford, is "now chiefly remembered for his romantic attachment to the Queen of Bohemia, daughter of James I.," was born in 1609, gained considerable renown for his military exploits while yet a youth, and having been closely attached to three monarchs, Charles I., Charles II., and James II., died an earl at the advanced age of eighty-eight years.

3. Ford, not always seen to an advantage in prologue or epilogue writing, is here at his best.

3: 11. *Commérce.* The common Elizabethan accent. One of the rules for accentuation then followed is thus laid down by Ben Jonson : "All verbs (and nouns derived from them) coming from the Latin, either of the supine or otherwise, hold the accent as it is found in the first person present of those Latin verbs."

3: 15. *Fiction.* The quarto reads *a fiction.*

4. The following quaint characterization of the various personages in the play is used by Ford in the original edition. He calls it : "The Speaker's names, fitted to their Qualities."

Amyclas, Common to the Kings of Laconia.
Ithocles, Honour of Loveliness.
Orgilus, Angry.
Bassanes, Vexation.
Armostes, an Appeaser.
Crotolon, Noise.
Prophilus, Dear.
Nearchus, Young Prince.
Tecnicus, Artist.
Hemophil, Glutton.
Groneas, Tavern-haunter.
Amelus, Trusty.
Phulas, Watchful.
Calantha, Flower of Beauty.
Penthea, Complaint.
Euphranea, Joy.
Christalla, Crystal.
Philema, a Kiss.

Grausis, Old Beldam.
*Persons included.*
Thrasus, Fierceness.
Aplotes, Simplicity.

**5.** The opening scene between Orgilus and his father, Crotolon, is admirable, in that we have set before us at the very outset the relation that so many of the principal actors in the drama bear toward one another.

**5 : 8.** *Areopagite.* "Member of the highest judicial court at Athens. Its sessions were held on Mars' Hill." (*Webster.*)

**6 : 18.** *Broached.* Let out, give vent to. The quarto has *brauch't* which Weber erroneously renders "transfixed."

**6 : 29.** *Convérse.* See **3 : 11.**

**7 : 65.** *Resolve.* Is determined, convinced.

**7 : 67.** *Sort.* Come about, fall out.

> I am glad that all things *sort* so well.
> *Much Ado about Nothing.* V. iv. 7.

**8 : 87.** Compare with Laertes' advice to Ophelia : *Hamlet,* Act I. sc. iii. Of this interview between brother and sister Gifford says : " Orgilus seems to entertain some suspicion of Ithocles ; but the exaction of such a promise appears not altogether consistent in one who had just been describing the misery of his own sufferings from the power and influence of a brother."

**9 : 109.** *Contents.* Contentedness, satisfaction.

**10 : 118.** *Change fresh airs.* Orgilus evidently does not believe in " change of air " as a cure for mental illness.

**11 : 35.** Ithocles, as he appears in the play, is hardly the man the words of Orgilus in the opening scene would lead us to expect. Experience seems to have tempered his ambition, and while he is still self-centered and masterful, it is clear that regret for his " pride of power " has effected a change for the better in his character.

**13 : 66.** *Provincial garland.* A wreath of honor which the ancients bestowed upon those who added a province to the empire.

**13 : 83.** *Voicing.* Proc

**14 : 89.** *Fit slights.* Trifling, slight services, referred to in befittingly humble terms. Ithocles here shows a modesty that is scarcely anticipated after Orgilus' description of him.

**16**: 134. *Thrum.*  Weave.  Thrum literally is the tufted end of weavers' threads.

> "O Fates, come, come, cut thread and *thrum.*"
> *Midsummer Night's Dream*, V. 291.

**17**: 1. Compare Tecnicus with Friar Lawrence in *Romeo and Juliet.*

**17**: 6. *Aspect.*  See **3** : 11.

**18** : 37. *Secure.*  Certain, sure.

**19** : 52. *Niceness.*  Prudishness :  viz., "in starting trivial and unimportant objections."  (*Gifford.*)

**21** : 92. *Tenters.*  A frame with hooks for stretching and drying cloth that has been wet or dyed.

**21** : 97. *Oratory.*  Study.

**21** : 102. Orgilus puts on this fantastic air to avert suspicion. His words are not a bad satire upon the sometimes ingenious but always over-wrought speeches of the euphuists of Elizabeth's day. See Osric, *Hamlet*, Act V. sc. ii.

**22** : 116. *Mew.*  "A term of the schools, used when false conclusions are illogically deduced from an opponent's premises." (*Gifford.*)

**22** : 125. *Grammates.*  This may be a sneering term referring to grammar.  *Taste the grammates* would seem to mean "get the slightest knowledge of the simplest facts."

**25** : 1. It is quite possible that by exaggerating the infirmity of Bassanes Ford thought to throw the patience, purity, and loveliness of Penthea into stronger relief.  We can excuse the dramatist for the coarse language which he puts into the mouth of the jealous husband, knowing how the standards of our time and those of the seventeeth century differ, but we can hardly overlook the sudden and wholly unexpected change which, a little later, comes over this ridiculous and revolting character.  The sudden transformation from absurd jealousy to doting fondness is scarcely conceivable.

**25** : 12. *Springal.*  Youth.

**26** : 26. *Cull.*  Embrace.

**26** : 45. *Mewed.*  Shed, moulted.  A falconer's term.

**27** : 69. *Pearls.*  A dissyllable.

**29 : 113.** *Goodly gear.* Matter.

> Here's *goodly gear.*
>
> *Romeo and Juliet,* II. iv. 107.

**30 : 125.** *Collops.* Small pieces of flesh.

**30 : 129.** *Caroches.* Coaches.

**31 : 134.** *Tympany.* From the Greek word meaning kettle-drum. It is here used to signify a sense of confusion.

**31 : 148.** *Railed at the sins.* The original reading which was changed by Gifford to " saints," and thus retained by Dyce.

**32 : 3.** *Seelèd dove.* A dove that has been blinded by sewing the eyelids. This wanton inhumanity was once regarded as sport. The dove, as described in the text, would, on being loosed, soar upward until exhausted, and then fall lifeless to the earth.

**32 : 12.** *It physics not, etc.,* Compare with *Macbeth,* V. iv. 40.

**33 : 22.** *Meat.* Gifford conjectures " bait."

**34 : 52.** *Extremes.* The quarto reads " extremities."

**34 : 55.** *Current.* An expression common with the old dramatists. So above, Act I. scene ii. line 84.

**35 : 80.** *Demur.* Delay.

**37 : 118.** *Whoreson.* An adjective applied not only to persons, but to anything, as a term of reproach or dislike.

**38 : 5.** This line is slightly corrupted. Weber reads :

> *To such alacrity as once his nature.*

**39 : 20.** It is impossible for Orgilus to disguise his admiration and passion even under the affected language of the schoolmen. Penthea, however, is not suspicious of his identity, attributing his words not to any subtle intention, but rather to wild vagary. Her whole attitude throughout this trying interview is one that commands the highest admiration, and awakens the deepest pity as well. Torn as her bosom is with conflicting emotions, it is the wife, to whom honor above all else is sacred, who speaks in every word.

**39 : 30.** *On Vesta's altars.* A badly mutilated passage amended by Gifford. The original is hopelessly confused, as will be seen by the following :

> " As the incense smoking
> The holiest altars, virgin tears (like
> On Vesta's odours) sprinkled dews to feed 'em,
> And to increase," etc.

**41 : 76.** *Borrowed shape.* Stock theatrical term for dress of disguise.

**43 : 124.** *Politic French.* An amusing anachronism.

**44 : 133.** *Aches.* A dissyllable.

**44 : 134.** *Imposthumes.* Swellings, inward sores.

> This is the *imposthume* of much wealth and peace,
> That inward breaks and shows no cause without
> Why the man dies.
> > *Hamlet*, IV. iv. 27.

**44 : 135.** *Humours.* Temper.

**44 : 149.** *Then let us care.* The quarto gives this speech to Bassanes, but manifestly it belongs to Penthea, being a continuation of her train of thought which is broken in upon by her husband.

**46 : 3.** *Jealous.* Suspicious, as frequently.

**47 : 43.** *Intrenching on.* Trenching upon.

**49 : 1.** Due praise has never been bestowed upon Ford's lyrical faculty. Aside from Shakespere and Beaumont and Fletcher, none of the old dramatists as a whole excels him. Webster wrote one dirge which Ford never equaled, but the latter's note is more natively lyrical. The song at the opening of this scene, and that in Act IV. scene iii., may be cited as admirable examples of his art. To these might be added the following from *The Lover's Melancholy*, Act II. scene i.:

SONG.

> Fly hence, shadows, that do keep
> Watchful sorrows charmed in sleep !
> Though the eyes be overtaken,
> Yet the heart doth ever waken
> Thoughts, chained up in busy snares
> Of continual woes and cares :
> Love and griefs are so exprest
> As they rather sigh than rest.
> Fly hence, shadows, that do keep
> Watchful sorrows charmed in sleep !

**51 : 33.** This scene between brother and sister is one of the strongest in the drama. The remorse of Ithocles at the sight of Penthea's suffering is rendered the more poignant by the realiza-

tion of his own apparently hopeless love.  Penthea, while she can
not refrain from reminding her brother that he is the cause of her
sorrows, shows her forgiving and sympathetic nature in the way in
which she espouses his interests.

**50 : 43.** *Spleen.*  A word in much more common use in Ford's
day than in our own, sometimes indicating impetuosity, eagerness,
sometimes caprice, and sometimes hate or malice.

**52 : 53.** *Affections.*  Sorrows.

**53 : 87.** *Turtles.*  Turtle-doves.  The turtle-dove was the em-
blem of faithful love.

**53 : 93.** *Nearness.*  This word does not occur in the original.  It
was suggested by Gifford as probably conveying the idea Ford
had in mind.

**54 : 111.** *I sweat in blood for't.*  An excusable bit of hyperbole,
considering the speaker's over-wrought state of mind.

**55 : 123.** *Property.*  "A thing quite at our disposal, and to be
treated as we please." (*Stevens.*)

> Do not talk of him
> But as a *property.*
>  *Julius Cæsar*, IV. i. 40.

**55 : 131.** *Progress.*  " This passage is not without curiosity as
tending to prove that some of the words now supposed to be
Americanisms were in use among our ancestors, and crossed the
Atlantic with them.  It is not generally known that Ford's
county, Devonshire, supplied a very considerable number of the
earlier settlers in the colonies." (*Gifford.*)

**55 : 144.** *Springal.*  Youthful.  See **25 : 12.**

**56 : 149.** *Franks.*  The figure is taken from the word " frank "
which means a small enclosure in which boars were fattened.

**56 : 155.** *Megrims.*  Whims, fancies.  *Firks*=freaks.

**57 : 167.** *Pandora's box.*  Pandora was, according to Greek
mythology, the first created female.  The story of her having been
the cause of the introduction of evil into the world is thus told by
Anthon : " Jupiter, incensed at Prometheus for having stolen the
fire from the skies, resolved to punish men for this daring deed.
He therefore directed Vulcan to knead earth and water, to give it
human voice and strength, and to make it assume the fair form of
a virgin like the immortal goddesses.  He desired Minerva to

endow her with artist knowledge, Venus to give her beauty, and Mercury to inspire her with an imprudent and artful disposition. When formed she was attired by the Seasons and Graces, and each of the deities having bestowed upon her the commanded gifts, she was named Pandora (all-gifted). Thus furnished, she was brought by Mercury to the dwelling of Epimetheus, who, though his brother Prometheus had warned him to be on his guard, and to receive no gifts from Jupiter, dazzled with her charms, took her into his house and made her his wife. The evil effects of this imprudent step were speedily felt. In the dwelling of Epimetheus stood a closed jar which he had been forbidden to open. Pandora, under the influence of female curiosity, disregarding the injunction, raised the lid, and all the evils hitherto unknown to man poured out, and spread themselves over the earth. In terror at the sight of these monsters, she shut down the lid just in time to prevent the escape of Hope, which thus remained to man his chief support and comfort." The source of this account is Hesiod.

**58 : 206.** This line was amended by Gifford. The original reads

To outdo art, and *cry a jealousy.*

**59 : 13.** Nearchus is a fair type of the noble suitor whose presence is necessary for the development of the plot, but whose part is as difficult as it is thankless, for Calantha openly snubs him at the first opportunity.

**60 : 34.** *Marriage.* A trisyllable.

**60 : 36.** *Tastes of.* An expression that has passed from use, though " savours " in the same sense is still not uncommon.

**61 : 44.** This meeting between Ithocles and Orgilus is exceedingly well carried out, the former really desiring to make amends in so far as possible for the wrong done in the past, the latter for his own hidden purposes veiling his hatred and appearing to meet his enemy halfway.

**61 : 59.** *Engrossed.* Mastered.

**63 : 19.** *Condition.* Disposition.

**63 : 21.** While in the preceding speech Orgilus refers to bygone injuries, it is only here that he allows his deep resentment to flame forth for a moment, so complete a command has he over himself.

**65**: 58. *Smooth.* Kindly.

**67**: 7. Penthea, in this most touching scene, seems to have a clear presage of her impending fate. It is indeed a bold stroke, the " bequeathing," as she puts it, of her brother to Calantha, but it proves successful, as the outcome shows, though at the time Calantha must needs hide her real thoughts by calling in her waiting women. Penthea's plea for Ithocles is a most moving appeal of a noble and forgiving mind that is upon the verge of being forever darkened.

**68**: 42. *Beshrew.* Originally a very mild term of imprecation, though occasionally used in a stronger sense.

**68**: 43. *Thou turns't me too much woman.* Shakespere twice makes use of " woman " in the same sense :

> *Wolsey.* Cromwell, I did not think to shed a tear
> In all my miseries ; but thou hast forced me,
> Out of thy honest truth, *to play the woman.*
> > *Henry VIII,* III. ii. 429–431.

> *Laertes.* Too much of water hast thou, poor Ophelia,
> And therefore I forbid my tears. But yet
> It is our trick ; nature her custom holds,
> Let shame say what it will ; when these are gone,
> *The woman will be out.*
> > *Hamlet,* IV. vii. 184–188.

**69**: 62. One of Ford's finest lines.

**72**: 4. *I am not what you doubt me.* What you suspect me to be.

**72**: 15. *A man of single meaning.* One without deceit, open, sincere.

**73**: 21. . . . *grace my hopes with any instance*
    *Of livery.*

That is, bestow upon me some mark of your favour.

Gifford is of the opinion that this expression was derived from the fact that the retainers of great families were accustomed to wear badges, upon which the crests of their respective houses were emblazoned or stamped.

**74 : 34.** *On't.* Of it. A common contraction more euphonious than of 't.

**74 : 38.** *Contents.* See **9** : 109.

**74 : 44.** *Increments.* Augmentation, increase.

**75 : 69.** As a punishment for his temerity, Ixion was hurled by Jupiter into Erebus, and there fastened to an ever-revolving wheel.

**76 : 82.** *Your.* An appelative.

**76 : 87.** *Fustian.* The word here has a meaning akin to smoothness. Velveteen is sometimes called "fustian," hence, perhaps, the figure.

**76 : 88.** *Less.* This word does not occur in the quarto. It was inserted by Gifford as necessary to the sense.

**77 : 102.** *Colt.* This was a term not infrequently applied in Ford's time to those in whom rudeness and folly were combined. It is quite possible that the dramatist may here have had in mind some tapestry, or "painted cloth," upon which he had seen represented the very figures he mentions.

**77 : 116.** "The extraordinary success with which the revengful spirit of Orgilus is maintained through every scene is highly creditable to the poet's skill. There is not a word spoken by him which does not denote a deep and dangerous malignity, couched in the most sarcastic and rancorous language. The bitterness of gall, the poison of asps, lurk under every compliment, which nothing but the deep repentance and heartfelt sincerity of Ithocles could possibly prevent him from feeling and detecting." (*Gifford.*)

**77 : 118.** *Suppling.* The quarto has *supplying.* At best the figure is somewhat confused.

**78 : 120.**         *The hurts are yet but mortal*
        *Which shortly will prove deadly.*

Gifford is of the opinion that for "*yet but*" we should read "*yet not.*" If, however, we take "*mortal*" in the sense of "*serious*" such a change will not be necessary.

**78 : 126.** *Saw.* Saying.

**78 : 141.** *I am not Œdipus.* The reference here is to the solution by Œdipus of the riddle propounded by the Sphinx which Juno had sent to ravage the territory of Thebes. For the story of Œdipus in full see Greek mythology.

**80 : 14, 15.** *Honeycomb of Honesty, Garland of Good-will.* Popular miscellanies containing stories, anecdotes, and songs. The latter appeared in 1631.

**80 : 17.** *Moil:* Mule.

**80 : 24.** *Quintessence.* A term much used by alchemists. The fifth essence which the Greeks who were followers of Pythagoras added to the four recognized elements, fire, air, water, and earth.

**81 : 54.** *Practice.* Try my patience.

**81 : 58.** This scene should be compared with *Hamlet,* Act. IV. scene iv.

**82 : 69.** Dyce thinks there is a slight corruption in the text here.

**82 : 71.** *Turtle.* See **52 : 87.**

**83 : 99.** *Whining gray dissimulation.* So Milton in *Paradise Regained :*

> He ended here ; and Satan, bowing low
> *His gray dissimulation—*

**83 : 100.** *Show justice, etc.* Orgilus here loses control over his feelings, and shows openly the intensity of his hatred, though Ithocles appears to think the words are addressed to Bassanes.

**83 : 103.** *Antic rapture.* Foolish passion. Possibly there may be some reference to the stage rant of the jealous husband or lover.

**83 : 105.** *Motion.* Puppet, image.

**84 : 111.** *My heart too.* A corruption in the text, one or more lines having been dropped.

**84 : 119.** *Points.* Tagged laces.

**84 : 125.** This line shows that whatever Orgilus may have had in mind up to this time, however he may have hesitated, all doubts and scruples, if he entertained any, are cast aside. From this point he is settled in his deadly determination, and there is no wavering in his line of action.

**85 : 144.** *O, my wrecked honour, etc.* Though one may not altogether agree with Gifford's view, his comments upon this speech of Penthea's are not without interest. " The transition of Penthea from the wandering insanity which had marked the previous part of her discourse to the deep but composed melancholy of what follows, is surely too sudden and may seem to throw some suspicion on the reality, not of her sufferings and despair, for these are too strongly marked for doubt, but of her abberration of mind ; and indeed it cannot be concealed that this lovely and interesting woman has a spice of selfishness in her grief, and approaches somewhat too nearly to Orgilus in the unforgiving part of his character.　Even her last words are expressive of resentment."

**89 : 6.** *Delphos.*　The oracle at Delphi was one of the three most celebrated in Greece, and was consulted upon all important occasions.　The oracular responses were delivered by the Pythia (priestess) after she had inhaled the vapor arising from the sacred cave or fissure.　The customary ambiguity of oracular prediction is well preserved by Ford in the prophecy that follows.　In order that the veracity of the deity might not be impeached, the priest (or priestess) took care that every statement made by the oracle should be susceptible of a double meaning.

**94 : 129.** Ithocles is too wrapped up in his own happiness to dream of anything save perfect frankness and friendliness in Orgilus, who, in this scene, with great subtleness draws his doomed enemy into his toils.

**95.**　The *engine* mentioned in the stage directions was simply an ordinary chair to which two movable arms were attached.　Ford, like the author of *The Devil's Charter*, Barnaby Barnes, who employs the same mechanism, doubtless got it from one of the tales of the Italian writer Bandello.

**97 : 25.** Ford's mythology here is apparently of his own invention.　The sisters of Phaëton, three (or seven) in number, were so grieved at the death of their brother that they were changed into poplars on the bank of the river into which the ill-fated youth fell.

**97 : 29.** *Turtle.*　Turtle-dove, as before.

**97 : 39.** The courage with which Ithocles meets his fate is as truly Spartan as the heroism of Calantha in the following act. The contrast between his calm acceptance of death and the bitterly revengeful spirit which Orgilus has up to this point harbored is a fine stroke on Ford's part.　Ithocles in a moment is transformed into a hero, and we see him towering over his executioner in nobility of character, forgiveness putting revenge to shame.

**97 : 42.** *Tent.*　Widen, probe.

**100 : 13.** *Splay-footed.* Spread-footed, having an abnormally flat foot. Some of the omens here enumerated were, in Ford's time, held in superstitious dread not only by the ignorant but also by the more learned.

**101 : 36.** *Index.* The index hand ( ☞ ) which was often used upon the margin of old books to call special attention to some passage or paragraph.

**101 : 42.** *Resolute.* Assured.

**102.** Hazlitt is of the opinion that the second scene of this act was suggested by the mask scene in Marston's *Malcontent.*

**105 : 48.** *Abiliment.* Ability.

**105 : 49.** *Fie, Orgilus !* The word *fie* must formerly have had a stronger meaning than at the present day else this exclamation, and the one which follows, would be nothing short of ridiculous.

**105 : 54.** *Convinced.* Refuted.

**107 : 100.** " In performing the operation of bleeding, formerly so common, the arm was bound above the spot selected in order to distend the veins. For the same reason the patient grasped a staff." (*Ellis.*)

**108 : 109.** *Fillet.* An unusual but striking use of the word.

**108 : 109.** *Grammercy.* Literally many thanks. (F. *grand-merci.*) An exclamation usually indicative of surprise.

**109 : 125.** *Broached.* See **6 : 18.**

**109 : 142.** *Cunning.* Skill in arms.

**110 : 155.** The dignity with which Orgilus meets his end can hardly fail to command our respect, if not our admiration. However much we may censure him for his malignant and unforgiving spirit, when once his revenge is accomplished his demeanor takes on a tinge of something exalted.

**110.** The *recorders* mentioned in the stage directions for the third scene of this act, were instruments similar to the flute.

" I do not know where to find in any play a catastrophe so grand, so solemn, and so surprising as this [of *The Broken Heart*]. This is indeed, according to Milton, to ' describe high passions and high actions.' The fortitude of the Spartan boy who let a beast gnaw out his bowels till he died, without expressing a groan, is a faint bodily image of this dilaceration of the spirit and exenteration of the inmost mind, which Calantha with a holy violence against her nature keeps closely covered, till the last duties of a wife and a queen are ful-

filled. Stories of martyrdom are but of chains and the stake; a little bodily
suffering ; these torments

> On the purest spirits prey
> As on entrails, joints, and limbs,
> With answerable pains, but more intense.

What a noble thing is the soul in its strength and in its weaknesses ! Who
would be less weak than Calantha? Who can be so strong? The expression
of this transcendent scene almost bears me in imagination to Calvary and the
Cross ; and I seem to perceive some analogy between the scenical sufferings
which I am here contemplating, and the real agonies of that final completion
to which I dare no more than hint a reference."

                                                    *—Charles Lamb.*

" Of all last scenes on any stage, the last scene of this play is the most over-
whelming in its unity of outward effect and inward impression. Other tragic
poems have closed as grandly, with as much or more of moral and poetic
force ; none, I think, with such solemn power of spectacular and spiritual
effect combined. As a mere stage show it is so greatly conceived and so tri-
umphantly wrought out, that even with less intense and delicate expression,
with less elaborate and stately passion in the measure and movement of the
words, it would stamp itself on the memory as a durable thing to admire ;
deep-based as it is on solemn and calm emotion, built up with choice and
majestic verse, this great scene deserves even the extreme eulogy of its greatest
critic."

                                        *—Algernon Charles Swinburne.*

**114 : 82, 83.** Lines four and five of the Dirge, which deserves
considerable praise, were slightly amended by Gifford.

# English Readings for Students.

This collection is planned to supply English master-pieces in editions at once competently edited and inexpensive. The aim will be to fill vacancies now existing because of subject, treatment, or price. The volumes will be of convenient size and serviceably bound.

## Coleridge: Prose Extracts.

Selections chosen and edited with introduction and notes by HENRY A. BEERS, Professor in Yale College. xxix + 148 pp. 16mo. Boards. Teachers' price, 30 cents ; postage 4 cents additional.

The selections, varying in length from a paragraph to ten or twenty pages, will be mainly from *Table Talk* and *Biographia Literaria*, but also in part from *The Friend*, *Notes on Shakspeare*, and other writings. They have been chosen, so far as may be, to illustrate the range and variety of Coleridge's thought, and, to emphasize this purpose, have been grouped by subjects. The introduction briefly summarizes the author's intellectual position and influence.

## De Quincey: Joan of Arc and The English Mail Coach.

Edited with an introduction and notes by JAMES MORGAN HART, Professor in Cornell University. xxvi + 138 pp. 16mo. Boards. Teachers' price, 30 cents ; postage 4 cents additional.

These essays have been chosen as fairly representative of the two most notable phases of the author's work, and as at the same time attractive to the novice in literary study. The introduction sketches the leading facts of De Quincey's life, and indicates some of the prominent

features of his style.   Allusions and other points of unusual difficulty are explained in the notes.   This volume
and the one containing the Essays on *Boswell's Johnson*
(see below) are used at Cornell University as foundation
for elementary rhetorical study.

## Dryden : Select Plays.

Edited with a brief introduction and notes by JAMES W. BRIGHT,
Assistant Professor in the Johns Hopkins University.   About 100
pp.   16mo.   [*In preparation.*]

Aside from their representing the principal literary ac-
tivity, in point of quantity, of one of the foremost English
writers, Dryden's plays have a peculiar interest in having
been among the first to be played upon the reopening of
the theatres under Charles II.

## Goldsmith : Present State of Polite Learning.

Edited with introduction and notes by J. M. HART, Professor in
Cornell University.   About 100 pp.   16mo.   [*In preparation.*]

There are many reasons, some of them obvious, for
giving this essay a place in the English Readings series.
One that may be mentioned is the remarkably clear
insight it affords into the entire eighteenth-century way
of criticising.   The introduction and notes will direct
the student's attention along this line of observation.

## Lyly : Endimion.

With introduction and notes by GEORGE P. BAKER, Instructor in
Harvard College.   16mo, pp. cxcvi + 109.

Lyly's plays really show him to a better advantage than
does the *Euphues*, by which he is chiefly remembered,
and his place in English dramatic history makes it de-
sirable that one at least should be easily accessible.

## Macaulay and Carlyle: Croker's Boswell's Johnson.

> The complete essays, with brief notes and an introduction by JAMES MORGAN HART, Professor in Cornell University. A preliminary edition, without notes, is now supplied. 93 pp. 12mo. Boards. Teachers' price, 30 cents ; postage 4 cents additional.

These parallel treatments of Croker's editing, and of the characters of Boswell and Dr. Johnson, afford an unusual opportunity for comparative study. The two essays present a constant contrast in intellectual and moral methods of criticism which cannot fail to turn the attention of students to important principles of biographical writing, while equally important principles of diction are impressively illustrated in the two strongly marked styles. The essays also offer an excellent introduction to the study of the literary history of Johnson's times.

## Marlowe: Edward II. With the best passages from TAMBURLAINE THE GREAT, and from his POEMS.

> With brief notes and an introductory essay by EDWARD T. McLAUGHLIN, Professor in Yale College.

Aside from the intrinsic value of *Edward II.*, as Marlowe's most important work, the play is of great interest in connection with Shakespere. The earlier chronicle drama was in Shakespere's memory as he was writing *Richard II.*, as various passages prove, and a comparison of the two plays (sketched in the introduction) affords basis for a study in the development of the Elizabethan drama. Since *Tamburlaine* has really no plot and character-development, extracts that illustrate its poetical quality lose nothing for lack of a context. The unobjectionable beginning of *Hero and Leander* is perhaps the finest narrative verse of the sixteenth century.

## Specimens of Argumentation. I. CLASSIC.

Chosen and edited by GEORGE P. BAKER, Instructor in English in Harvard College, and Non-resident Lecturer on Argumentative Composition in Wellesley College. [*In preparation.*]

## Specimens of Argumentation. II. MODERN.

Chosen and edited by GEORGE P. BAKER. 16mo. 186 pp. Boards.

This compilation includes Lord Chatham's speech on the withdrawal of troops from Boston, Lord Mansfield's argument in the Evans case, the first letter of Junius, the first of Huxley's American addresses on evolution, Erskine's defence of Lord George Gordon, and an address of Beecher's in Liverpool during the cotton riots. The choice and editing has been controlled by the needs of the courses in " Forensics" in Harvard College. The earlier selections offer excellent material for practice in drawing briefs, a type of such a brief being given in the volume. The notes aim to point out the conditions under which each argument was made, the difficulties to be overcome, and wherein the power of the argument lies. It is thought that the collection, as a whole, will be found to contain available illustrations of all the main principles of argumentation, including the handling of evidence, persuasion, and scientific exposition.

HENRY HOLT & CO., PUBLISHERS, NEW YORK.

CPSIA information can be obtained
at www.ICGtesting.com
Printed in the USA
BVHW072317051218
534639BV00052B/630/P